What are People Saying About This Book?

A nice contrast from the other Project Management materials currently used in the classrooms and workplace, [...] Kozak-Holland takes the blandness of the PMBoK and combines it with a story.

- TCM Reviews

Straightforward and to the point, [...] once I started reading, I found that I could not put the book down.

- Ed Snowden, PMP, Project Manager, Ontario's Workplace Safety and Insurance Board

I found Mark's most recent book to be quite excellent. His ability to apply project management theory and methodologies to historical events is quite unique and informative.

- Thomas Clement, HP Education Services

Exciting, pertinent, and fun. Mark Kozak-Holland takes a great (and true) story and makes the connection to today's project management challenges. A great read and lessons learned of the best kind. A must read for PMs.

- Kevin Reynolds, Project Management Senior Instructor, ESI International

A tremendous resource for educators. The stark reality of failed projects and Mark's detailed research, historical accuracy, and the link to the PMBoK help us to analyze and understand that we are not alone in managing our complex projects today. The incredible resourcefulness and bravery of these men gives us hope on our own troubled projects.

- Linda F. Desmond, PMP, President of the PMI Mass Bay Chapter

[Author Mark Kozak-Holland] has taken a series of events and honorably translated them into a book that shows how project planning works. [...] His ability to teach the subject by using historic events is second to none. Mr. Kozak-Holland has provided business managers, college students, and anyone interested in the subject a series of books that needs to be part of every college, university, and library. If you haven't read his books, I strongly recommend that you do. They are excellent, and "Project Lessons from the Great Escape" is no exception.

- William E. Cooper in *Reader Views*

Project Lessons from The Great Escape (Stalag Luft III)

Author
Mark Kozak-Holland

First Edition

Multi-Media
Publications Inc.
Oshawa, Ontario

Project Lessons from The Great Escape
By Mark Kozak-Holland

Acquisitions Editor:	Kevin Aguanno
Copy Editor:	Josette Coppola
Typesetting:	Tak Keung Sin
Cover Design:	Cheung Hoi

Published by:
Multi-Media Publications Inc.
Box 58043, Rosslynn RPO, Oshawa, Ontario, Canada, L1J 8L6

http://www.mmpubs.com/

ISBN (Paperback):   1-895186-80-3
ISBN (PDF edition):   1-895186-81-1

Published in Canada.

Library and Archives Canada Cataloguing in Publication

Kozak-Holland, Mark

Project lessons from the Great Escape (Stalag Luft III) / author, Mark Kozak-Holland. --1st ed.

(Lessons from history)
Includes bibliographical references.
Also available in electronic format.
ISBN 1-895186-80-3

1. Project management. 2. Prisoner-of-war escapes--Poland--Zaga'n. 3. Tunneling. I. Title. II. Series: Lessons from history.

HD69.P75K686 2007   658.4'04   C2006-906992-1

Table of Contents

Acknowledgments

I am indebted to many chapters of the Project Management Institute™ for hosting the "Lessons from History" speaking series. These events led to numerous conversations with project managers who brought forth comments and ideas about their own "historical projects." As a result, I started to think about what a project essentially is. The initial idea for the Great Escape occurred to me a few years ago, and as I compared it to other "Lessons from History" projects, it really stuck out in my mind. This is primarily because this project started off in a hostile environment, it had no resources, and it was being continually shut down. How could it ever be successful?

I would like to thank Kevin Aguanno for helping me to pull this book together and for providing his usual sound advice and guidance.

I am incredibly indebted to my wife Sharon and my family (Nicholas, Jamie, and Evie), who have been so gracious in allowing me to continue with this writing project at the expense of our valuable time together.

If you have any ideas for improving this book, please contact me via e-mail. Your feedback can be incorporated into a future edition.

Mark Kozak-Holland

E-mail: mark.kozak-holl@sympatico.ca

Dedication

To my wife Sharon and children Nicholas, Jamie, and Evie.

Foreword

Lets turn back the time clock to sixty years ago. The setting is the briefing prior to a wartime operation. The senior RCAF Officer of 408 squadron was addressing the crews: "The targets tonight are the ball bearing factories in Schweinfurt, a high priority target for it is essential to demolish this key component and curtail German aircraft engine manufacturing production."

Some hours later, we were over the target, clearly marked by our Pathfinder Mosquitos, and had just released our bomb load from 25,000 feet, confirmed by our bomb aimer with "Bombs away." The antiaircraft fire was even more intense than the searchlights trying to cone our aircraft, with shrapnel clattering against our aircraft, and exploding shells all around us. The slipstreams from our own bombers were creating such turbulence that it was a very bumpy ride.

Suddenly, there was a stupendous explosion as cannon fire from a Messerschmitt struck our fuselage and killed our midupper gunner. From my navigator's position, behind the pilot, I watched in fascination as the fuel gauges unwound as the wing tanks emptied. Quickly, I realized that it was a mortal hit for our Lancaster so I notified Bus, our pilot to take a course change and head for Switzerland, since we would never have returned to Britain with only two functioning engines and since we were already losing altitude rapidly. A second attack some 15 minutes later inflicted further damage, and we heard the terse command from Bus: "Abandon aircraft, good luck."

Hitting the silk was a surreal experience – I still remember the sudden quiet as the chute opened, while below me I watched our aircraft spiraling down towards the ground. That was when the oscillations of the chute made me lose my egg – a very special treat in wartime England offered to aircrew before or on return from an operation. Mostly, we all opted to have it prior to takeoff; however, mine was now "*kaput*."

My entire life flashed through my mind despite trying to focus on what lay immediately ahead. The plane crashed and burst into flame, and I wondered how many of our remaining six crew members had survived. It took almost a year to find out the answer, as high winds had widely dispersed our chutes.

Some ten days later, I had been captured, passed through Dulag Luft, Frankfurt for interrogation, and dispatched to Stalag Luft III in Eastern Silesia (then a part of East Germany but now part of Poland). I was assigned a bunk in Hut 104 which was only 12 feet from the entrance to the tunnel named Harry but internal camp security was so tight that it was several weeks before I knew about this extraordinary, well-planned mass-escape attempt.

Incarceration is so depressing, especially in the traumatic early phase. Charles Morgan, essayist and prisoner of war from the First World War succinctly phrased it: "The doors may be slammed shut but the windows are open." The Luftwaffe was responsible for the camp and all air force POWs.

I found myself in a huge camp consisting of six compounds and 10,000 Allied Air Force Officers, all highly skilled, intelligent, and determined to make as much trouble for the Huns as possible by continually prodding for novel escapes. The camp was also a "League of Nations" with representatives from all the European nations Hitler's panzers had overrun, plus Canadians, Americans, Australians, New Zealanders, and South Africans. This plethora of languages allowed for excellent language training and the camp had established a virtual university that gave classes for a wide spectrum of subjects. The Germans encouraged this on the mistaken rationale that it would keep POWs occupied and not so concerned about escaping.

Congruent with this logic, the Germans allowed us to convert an unused barracks block into a 350 seat theatre. Prisoners turned the barracks into a theatre using the recycled plywood crates that contained the Canadian Red Cross food parcels, and received lumber, paints, and curtains for creating sets from the German guards.

We produced plays and musicals with such a level of improvised sophistication that the front row was always saved for invited German officers. This, in turn, opened opportunities for "legitimate" requests for a camera and film to record our productions. When the camera finally arrived, the escape committee was able to make photos for potential escapee passes, copy train timetables, and make maps to establish escape routes.

The escape committee was formed around a small group of dedicated and experienced would-be escapers under "Big X," Squadron Leader Roger Bushell, a South African lawyer who already had seven failed escape attempts. The escape committee was all powerful for in-camp security and assessed all escape proposals, backing those that had a modicum of success but discouraging ones that had not been carefully planned or that had little chance of getting a POW back to England.

The escape committee had decided to build three tunnels (referred to as Tom, Dick, and Harry) and had made progress in tunneling each. The major problem faced by the group was to find "innocent" ways to dispose of the excavated sand without German cognizance. This was done mainly by teams of men equipped with self-made long pockets inside their pants that could be filled with the lighter colored sand from 30 feet down. We called these men "penguins." A drawstring would allow the sand to escape so that it could be scuffed into a blend with surface sand.

Another difficulty was finding the timber to shore up the tunnel, for every foot had to be supported to preclude collapses. Again, the escape committee decreed that each POW would contribute a bed board from their bunk each time more supports were required.

The tunnel entrances were created with exquisite care. They were camouflaged and could be quickly closed off whenever German "ferrets" (those tasked with uncovering escape attempts) approached. Spotters meticulously monitored all Germans entering the camp and followed their every movement in the compound.

Wood was also found to build a trolley on rails that could convey diggers who were pulled by a rope to the face of the excavation. Likewise, excavated sand could be conveyed from the tunnel face back to the entrance chamber for hoisting to the surface and then dispersal. The process was refined until it was so efficient that digging could add another six to seven feet per day to the tunnel.

My own role in all of this was largely in the background, serving as a penguin and monitoring German guards or ferrets that entered the camp to ensure that they did not stumble onto any of our nefarious activities. I was also involved with the theatre.

Food was a constant problem as POWs were lowest on the list for rations. Initially, the Red Cross food parcels came regularly and each POW was assigned a parcel each week. Certainly, the food parcels saved a number of lives for much of the meager German food was rotten (I'm still psychologically unable to eat a turnip) or ersatz fish, a cheese created from fish products. This brings to mind my early Sagan days when I was given a tour by one of my New Zealander roommates of the other kriegies in hut 104. One room we entered had a human skeleton sitting in a chair and someone introduced me: "George, meet George – but please don't tell the Germans as we are still drawing his rations." Naively, I fell for it as everyone was so straight faced but it turned out to be a genuine human skeleton bought in Berlin for the half dozen POWs who were studying anatomy as part of their medical studies (regular exams were sent by London University and then passed back via the Swiss Red Cross). This is a good example of how important it was for POWs to retain a sense of humour despite the all-encompassing barbed wire, goon boxes armed with snipers, and constant patrolling by perimeter sentries.

Finally, the date for breaking open Harry was set at March 24. Deferment was not feasible as forged passes had to be dated or they would not pass scrutiny at German checkpoints. POWs felt tension, excitement, and anxiety as the countdown wore on. All of block 104 was judiciously evacuated, and 220 officers surreptitiously replaced them prior to blackout time. This was taking a chance that the Germans would not call a surprise check search on hut 104 – they had photo IDs of where each POW was billeted.

The weather had not cooperated for it was bitterly cold and a blizzard had dumped so much snow that escapee traveling "hard arser" cross-country would be much impeded. Another dilemma that delayed the breakout was a night raid on Berlin that evening – the power grid was cut for our Sagan region. The tunnel lighting system, contrived after light fingered POWs had swiped several reels of electric wire from inattentive workmen, was not functioning. The tunnel blackout meant smoky fat lamps had to be lit, else many escapees would succumb to claustrophobia. Some of the hard arsers were convinced the cold would be a problem so they wrapped an extra blanket around their girth; these men got stuck by the low ceiling of the tunnel and precious time was lost extricating them without dislodging the boards shoring up the roof.

The final disaster came with the realization that the tunnel was some ten feet short of the concealing woods and emerged at the edge of a roadway. Quickly, an answer was contrived to use a long rope so that each escapee could tug a jerk to signify that he had made it to the woods. At about 4 a.m., however, an armed sentry, patrolling the perimeter barbed wire, took an amble toward the woods to relieve himself. Suddenly, as he groped his pants open, a head popped up between his legs. The surprised sentry fired off his rifle to raise the alarm. The shot was heard throughout the camp and we realized the tunnel had been found. The game was up, and quickly squads of heavily-armed and trigger-happy goons occupied the camp. We were all forced out to the sports field and lined up facing machine guns as they tried to count us and find out how many had escaped. That took some six to eight hours as we stomped our feet in vain attempts to keep warm.

All privileges were suspended, food rations and water stopped, and all POWs were confined to barracks. Rumors were rampant but within a few days it was confirmed that 76 officers had escaped and that the Wehrmacht, police, SS, and Gestapo had mounted a massive manhunt across all of Germany.

All but three were recaptured. About two weeks
passed until the German Commandant met with our senior
British Officer to announce "We regret to inform you that all
of your comrades have been recaptured but fifty were trying to
re-escape and were shot". Our SBO, shocked, asked how many
had been wounded. The answer came back that all fifty had
died. All in our camp were so profoundly affected that we
expressed our grieving by sewing black armbands on our
tunics. The Germans ordered them removed but we did not
comply for we wanted that reminder of this atrocity to be
there for every *appel*.

Some two months later, there was another summons
by the Commandant who "regretfully" handed over the
cremated ashes of our fifty men. Life in camp was repressive;
many of the German guards appeared genuinely shocked but
did not criticize the action, maintaining that it was the SS or
Gestapo who were responsible. There was enough sympathy
that the Germans agreed to allow a small work party to go
outside the campgrounds and build a stone cairn so that the
ashes could be placed in a sheltered woodland grove.

Over the summer months, the war intensified but life
in camp regained some "normalcy:" sports were resumed, the
theatre reopened (my play had a full house), and classes and
lectures began again but the Red Cross parcels diminished to
one parcel per month and the German rations dropped ever
lower.

The Russians continued to advance with spectacular
successes. In mid January 1945, they were close to the camp.
We could see spotter planes and the artillery guns signified that

"liberation was at hand." Instead, the Russians halted to regroup at the Oder River which gave the Germans time to realize that POWs had potential as hostages. We were informed that we had ten hours to pack anything we could carry and then we'd be marched westward. Sure enough, early the next morning we were counted, paraded out of the camp, and joined the throngs of terrified refugees and retreating panzer and other military. It was total chaos with snow on the ground and frigid temperatures but we shuffled along, some towing primitive sleds to ease their burdens or to carry a sick POW. We were discouraged from bartering or even conversing with evacuees but soon the guards were tired and cold and did not notice that we were not obeying silly commands. At the end of our straggling column were several horse-drawn carts that picked up POWs too sick to continue.

We tried to sleep in the fields and, by about the third day, we were billeted in a glass factory that still had the furnaces going full blast. Oh, the joy of finally regaining some warmth! Many of us took our tin of margarine, placed it close to the molten glass and as soon it melted, drank the warmth down. It sounds sickening but it was a morale booster and it finally halted our desperate shivering. Some even managed to sleep.

Eventually, we reached a rail freight yard and were forced into wagons designed for holding eight horses but which were jammed with upwards of 125 men to each. This crowding created a small nest of body warmth but dictated few were able to lie down while the rest had to stand. The train stayed engineless for another day before a steam engine was attached and off we went.

We were sure that we'd get bombed by our own planes and that would be the finale to our war. Yet, somehow we survived, finally ending up near a condemned Navy camp close to Bremen. The camp was in a shambles and overrun by rats (which, within a few days, ended up adding some protein to our ubiquitous swede soup). What concerned us, though, was that we were close to a launch site for V2 rockets that were destined for demolishing London. We were sitting next to a prime target for the RAF.

Our stay at this site ended when the British crossed the Rhine. We were jubilant that we'd soon be free. Instead, the Germans announced another forced march, this time heading northeast toward the Baltic Sea. We refused to budge but again the SS appeared and their machine guns were convincing in getting us on the road again. It was early April and spring had arrived. Despite the chaos, bombings, and strafing we could barter cigarettes for food as the guards very lax, recognizing that the end of the war was close. One of my buddies traded three cigarettes for six fresh goose eggs. Upon camping in a field that night, we got a campfire blazing and had our resident chef serve up a memorable omelet, spiked with a tasty herb, stinging nettles. This was the first time in months – even years – that the 18 diners had tasted an egg. It was a delicious moment.

By the end of April, we had reached the outskirts of Stettin and were billeted on a huge Nazi bigwig's estate run by Polish and Russian "slaves." Finally, our liberation was upon us. It was almost an anticlimax when an armored vehicle, bearing British insignia, pulled into the farmyard. The turret door opened and our jubilant cheers greeted a pimply-faced soldier from General Montgomery's Cheshire Regiment. Freedom, what a feeling!

Within a few days, we had been deloused, had tossed our dirty, ragged tunics and trousers into the garbage, and had been issued new army uniforms. It was analogous to being born again.

So, how did the Great Escape and almost two years of being "behind the wire" set the pattern for my future? Despite the hardships and the fact I was down to 90 lbs. (I had extra rations once back in England and soon regained my health), the experiences had broadened my horizions and made me far more empathetic to human suffering. When I came home, I completed a science degree and took graduate work in education at McGill University. High school teaching supplied the motivation to step ahead with a Masters at Wesleyan in Connecticut. The opportunity to take a sabbatical spurred me to four years of cancer research and a Ph.D. at London University. Upon my return to Canada, I spent some 20 years in nursing education, which culminated, upon my retirement, in spending two years in Australia evolving problem-based learning for nursing.

Why does this book have such potential for the corporate world, government, and the military? I think it is because this book shows how to reach consensus using a team approach to strategic planning. The loyalty, tight security, creative solutions, and dearth of facilities that plagued POWs brought forth pragmatic but novel solutions to our project team. Basic too was the team members' steady persistence and constant focus on our goal.

Business acumen, like POW adaptability, evolves over time. It needs, however, some guidance – a template such as this – to guarantee high involvement from employees. With employees learning over time, business teams can reduce the need for supervision by decentralizing the firm's decision-making processes. Likewise, creating a high level of trust (the POWs knew their life was often in the hands of their colleagues) will enhance team decision-making processes.

In closing, permit me to share with you the perceptive words on the following page. This passage is dedicated to Sagan's Fifty & Others.

Dr George McKiel
Historical Advisor,
The Great Escape Memorial Project

Rank: Flight Lieutenant

Service: 4 wartime years + 2 yrs in the Special Mobilization Reserve

The War in the Air

For a saving grace, we didn't see our dead;
Who rarely bothered coming home to die
But simply stayed away out there
In the clean war, the war in the air.

Seldom the ghosts came back bearing their tales
Of hitting the earth, the incomprehensible sea,

But stayed up there in the relative wind,
Shades fading in the mind,

Who had no graves but only epitaphs
Where never so many spoke for never so few:
Per ardua, said the partisans of Mars,
Per aspera, to the stars.

That was the good war, the war we won
As if there were no death, for goodness sake,
With the help of the losers we left out there
In the air, in the empty air.

— *Howard Nemerov, novelist, critic, and poet*

Preface

Most of us have seen the movie *The Great Escape* (Metro Goldwyn Mayer™, 1963). This film has captivated audiences with its humour and action, but it has also falsely coloured our view of the actual event of 1944. No motorbikes were used in the escape, and the most exotic transportation the escapees could hope for was a train ride.

So how does this relate to the field of project management today? Many projects today are initiated with clear objectives, executive sponsorship, and healthy budgets, but they still fail. Other projects have no budgets and numerous obstacles in their way, and yet they succeed. This is the story of one of the perceived successes.

In my quest to find examples of great projects from history, I didn't immediately think of the Great Escape, as it did not follow the traditional blueprint of a construction project. Then I started thinking about projects that required a lot of planning, preparation, and teamwork, and it occurred to me that the Great Escape fell into this category. After some research, I discovered it had all the hallmarks of a great project: complex timelines, limited resources, dire circumstances, and hostile conditions. When I described the idea to several people, they immediately latched onto it. Well, of course they remembered the 1963 film, called the best war movie of all time. How can anyone forget the scenes of prisoners toiling in the tunnels, forging official-looking documents, and devising the cat-and-mouse early warning system Yet after further research, I learned that this isn't the whole story, and of course the movie was made by Hollywood many years ago, and historical accuracy was sometimes sacrificed for artistic considerations.

The Great Escape from the German prison camp Stalag Luft III is widely regarded as one of the most daring escape attempts of the twentieth century, so attention has generally been focused on its more sensational aspects. We can learn much more about the art of project management by examining instead the fundamental elements of the escape. During its development as an event in March of 1944, set in the grimmest of circumstances, what actually happened? How was the escape planned and executed as a project? How did it get around numerous obstacles in a habitat designed to be escape proof? How was the project tracked? In today's world, business people are also grappling with numerous obstacles in planning and executing projects in a climate of rapid change. What can be learned from this famous event of the past and put into practice today?

We know enough about the Great Escape to appreciate the extent of both its challenges and its accomplishments. Everything in Stalag Luft III was set up to prevent escape, and the project planning and preparation were hindered every day by new barriers created by the captors. The environment was ripe for a project failure, yet the escape committee (project team) was able to organise itself and get around every roadblock it encountered. Ideas and solutions were constantly tested and refined in a determined atmosphere where everything was believed to be possible. Throughout the project, no written project plan was ever produced, yet planning was done extensively. The escape committee overcame continuous difficulties and ran the project in an agile fashion. At one point the captors discovered the existence of an escape tunnel. This was a setback that should have completely shut down the project, but the escape mission continued to move forward because the advance planning included a contingency provision for this scenario.

Prisoners of War (POWs) spent twenty-four hours a day thinking about escape, but wishful thinking alone was not enough to ensure that the escape would be effective. Everything had to be thought through and assessed, including whatever could go wrong. Unfortunately, as with even the most meticulously planned projects, some things were overlooked, and this severely hampered the prison camp breakout. Learning how these oversights happened more than sixty years ago will help you with your projects today.

This book explores the ways in which the escape committee members, under tremendous pressure, inspired the inmates around them to continue a fight that many considered already lost. Everyone had to not only stave off hunger and psychological pressures but also deliver a project under the most trying of circumstances. For the escape committee, this meant understanding the problems facing them and focusing slender resources on critical tasks. It also meant unifying the camp POWs to work as a team on this one project, maximising that work effort, and matching individual skill sets with project activities. In a very short time, the escape committee transformed the camp POWs into an agile project team, one that could adapt to changing and unexpected daily situations by using the handcrafted, rudimentary technologies of the day.

As you go through this book, you will find many surprises, like the fact that the Great Escape encompassed everything we would face in a modern project today. I outline this commonality by stepping through the life cycle of the escape project and considering it in terms of the nine project management knowledge areas typical of projects today. This perspective does not only highlight how the escape committee managed integration, scope, time, cost, quality, human resources, communications, risk, and procurement. It also demonstrates how intuitively correct these knowledge areas are for a project.

Reading this book will help you manage your projects better. Consider whether you have ever faced a project with any of these features:

- Intimidating scope
- No resources
- No budget
- Intolerable time constraints
- New obstacles appearing every day
- Hostile groups trying to close down the project
- Stringent penalty systems
- Continuously changing environment

If you have encountered any of these problems within a project, then take heart. The escape committee faced all these issues, and "stringent penalty systems" for that project included the threat of death. The Great Escape of 1944 operated under the most difficult circumstances and was still able to achieve something remarkable, and so can you.

CHAPTER ONE

The Story Begins

"For you the war is over" were usually the first words a *captured airman heard.*[1]

T his chapter looks at why projects fail to start and why the fear of failure needs to be overcome. It gives the background to the journey of the team members (prisoners) who found themselves in captivity and discusses their states of mind.

Today's Project

How many times have you been faced with a project that is based on a good idea but has no official sanction? It lacks finances, resources, and sponsors, and everything is stacked against it. But you represent a group with an understanding of the problems and a vision to advance in the project, and you know that fundamentally this is the right thing to do. How do you get this project off the ground and turn it into a reality? Well, first you need to understand the difference between project success and project failure. Once you have done this, you can then take the first step in your project.

What Is Project Success?

Typically, project success means that project objectives or stakeholder expectations are met in the overall outcome.

What Is Project Failure?

Usually, project failure means that the stated project objectives or requirements are not met. A project could also be considered a failure if it does not deliver the expected value, does not meet stakeholder expectations, or results in general client dissatisfaction. But project failure is not simply the reverse of project success; for example, it could also be a sense of failure among team members.

Types of Project Failure

There are generally two types of project failure[2:]

1. **A project that consumes resources but fails to deliver an acceptable Return on Investment (ROI).**

   - The project is terminated before completion.

     - Needs cease to exist; for instance, the world changes unpredictably

34

- Decision makers have a change of heart or are replaced by ones who don't care about the project

- The project is poorly scoped, so resource allocation is insufficient as it develops

  - Necessary resources become insufficient or unavailable

- The project is incorrectly defined, resulting in low adoption or insufficient value

- The project produces no learning lessons

A project may deliver all of its promised services but yield performance that is not quite up to par. As a result, adoption rates are below expectations and the ROI suffers. Is this a success or a failure?

2. **A project that consumes resources but fails to deliver as proposed**

   - The project exceeds the budget

   - The project exceeds the time limit

   - The project doesn't meet the specifications

In this second category, a completed project does not materialise and deliver an acceptable ROI. The budgets and schedules that are exceeded have a severe impact on other areas of the business. There is no limit to the damage that a late, overspent, or underperforming project can cause to an organisation.

Yet failure—or the degree of it—is in the eye of the beholder, as it is a qualitative measure. A defense contractor that works for years on a cost-plus project may not consider it a failure just because the results are never put into service.

Fear of Project Failure

Some projects never get off the ground because of the fear of failure. The Project Management Office (PMO) determines that the risks are too high, and the project is put on hold. So how can the risks be reduced, and what can be done to make the project more palatable? For most project managers, experiencing some project failures is important as it provides a valuable firsthand "history lesson" on how to stay on track in future projects.

All the above factors are relevant to the Great Escape and will be revisited at the end of the story in "Chapter 8: Closing—Project Success or Failure."

The Story Begins

The story starts in Germany in March of 1943. At that point there were over 100,000 Allied airmen in captivity, many more than the Germans had expected. This sheer volume of prisoners was becoming a problem to them in terms of providing all the resources required. Although some of the captives were fighter pilots, the majority of airmen were from bomber crews. Typically, a bomber crew consisted of pilots, radio operators, navigators, and gunners from all walks of life and with differing skills. The average age of the Lancaster seven-man crew was only twenty-two years, and on average the Lancasters completed twenty-one missions before being lost.[3]

Figure 1.1: The Lancaster Bomber was the mainstay of RAF Bomber Command.

Changing Circumstances

Airmen usually found themselves in enemy hands very quickly, only hours after being in the comfort of their familiar surroundings: the company of their girlfriends, wives, and families; the mess hall; and the local pub.[4]

Figure 1.2: An Allied bomber crew getting briefed before a mission

One minute they were in the protection of their aircraft thousands of feet above the ground, and in the next they were landing into a strange and unfamiliar land. Suddenly they were at the mercy of the enemy, an unknown group of people, facing an uncertain fate. Airmen suffered the trauma of escaping by parachute from their badly-damaged aircraft and surviving the ordeal, all the while knowing that the rest of their crew may have died. They generally wore or carried their only possessions.

Figure 1.3: An Allied bomber getting shot down.

Being Prepared

Before taking off in their planes, airmen were issued an escape kit in case they were shot down over enemy territory. Each escape kit consisted of about $250 in currency to help in tight situations where bribes would be required, maps, condensed rations in tubes, and pills to keep the airmen awake whilst they were evading pursuit.

Figure 1.4: An Allied airman's escape/survival kit.

Avoiding Captivity

Airmen were encouraged to stay low to avoid capture and to establish contact with local resistance organisations scattered throughout Europe. By 1943 these organisations had well-established escape routes for airmen, and by use of these routes hundreds of airmen were delivered safely back to the United Kingdom every year.

Figure 1.5: An Allied airman shot down and captured.

Airmen would typically take the insignia off their uniforms, travel cross-country at night, and look for shelter during the day. Local *Wehrmacht* (German armed forces) types and the home guard were usually on the lookout for crashed airmen.

No Public Sympathy for Airmen

By the end of 1943, local German populations had developed a particular hatred for Allied airmen. The Allied aerial bombardment of the Third Reich reached a scale that was unprecedented, and the unfortunate victims of these bombings thought of the Allied airmen as *Luftgangsters* (terror fliers) and murderers of children and women. By the end of the war, even many of the Allied bomber crews themselves were beginning to have some misgivings about their deadly task. Because of this general outrage towards Allied airmen, a few were roughly handled by mobs after parachuting down near the cities they had been bombing.

Figure 1.6: Captured POWs brought into captivity.

43

Psychological Effects

The speed of the transition from freedom to captivity was not the only shock the airmen suffered. There were other traumatic factors, like the indefinite length of confinement, the difficult conditions, and the possibility of not coming out of the experience alive. The cumulative effect of all these stresses shocked the POWs into initially complying with their captors, and it was only after some time that their attitudes and behaviour began to change.

When taken into captivity, POWs were stripped, searched, and interrogated. They were confined in solitary cells for four or five days and denied Red Cross food, toilet articles, and cigarettes. Sometimes an uncooperative POW would be held in solitary for the full thirty days permitted by the Geneva Convention.

Figure 1.7: An Allied airman brought into the POW camp.

Coming to Terms with Captivity

It was a traumatic experience to be captured as a POW, a little like coming to terms with a serious illness or death. Typically, a prisoner's response to this trauma would go through five discrete phases (disbelief, anger, bargaining, depression, and acceptance), an emotional roller coaster that was riddled with doubts and uncertainties.

- **Disbelief:** Airmen were briefed about the possibility of sudden capture to give them time to prepare themselves for this contingency and take care of personal affairs at home. The state of disbelief did not last long as the reality of capture set in.

- **Anger:** Suddenly the airmen were not in control of their own lives. They felt angry and helpless at first, with anger directed primarily at the enemy but also at the other people around them.

- **Bargaining (willingness to compromise):** Airmen were typically suffering from insecurities about whether they would ever see their families again. Knowing this, the captors interrogated them and offered them deals.

- **Depression:** Awareness that imprisonment is inevitable for a long, indefinite time has a negative emotional impact. A normal part of incarceration is living a life with too much free time and constant uncertainty. The symptoms of prison life are simply impossible to ignore.

- **Acceptance:** This comes after working through the numerous conflicts and feelings that imprisonment brings and interacting with other POWs. As

they become weaker, wearier, and less emotional,
the prisoners gradually accept their fates as
inevitable and settle into a state of emotional
calmness.

The POWs realised that they were in a combat situation and
knew that the essential element for survival and success under
these wartime conditions was military discipline.

Conclusions

Many projects simply fail to get started due to the presence of
far too many obstacles, the perceived absence of resources, or
the fear of failure (usually based on high risk). In the prison
camps, the captives were put in a disadvantageous position and
intimidated into toeing the line rather than causing problems
for the authorities. For these POWs, the easiest response
would have been to resign themselves to the situation and drift
aimlessly through the war in captivity. The interrelationships
with other POWs were essential to prevent such a state of
malaise and apathy, and those who survived best were the most
mentally resilient.

Likewise, in today's world most obstacles to a project's
progress can be overcome if there is a determination to
succeed. There has to be an inner belief in the success of the
project. This winning state of mind begins by convincing the
people around you that any difficulties can be conquered and
the project can achieve its objectives.

CHAPTER TWO

Background and Environmental Situation

"There are 850 officer POWs in this camp. Half the buggers intend to lie on their backs dreaming of the past, improving their education, and writing nice letters home to Mom, or their girlfriend, and waiting until the war ends. The war might last for five or ten or twenty years. I do not intend to spend the rest of my life doing that and existing on one ersatz German beer a year. I'm getting out." - Wally Floody, Chief of Tunnel Engineering[5]

This chapter looks at the background and conditions in which the project originated and the impact of a hostile environment. It also discusses the players in the project, their backgrounds, and their relationships to each other.

Location of the Camp

Stalag Luft III was built to hold some of the finest escape artists in the Allied Air Forces, POWs with an escape record. It was a purposely bleak, inhospitable POW camp built inside the northern edge of a sandy pine forest that stretched for more than twenty miles. Located near Sagan in eastern Germany (now Poland), it was 105 miles (160 kilometers) from Berlin, 80 miles (130 kilometers) from Dresden, over 400 miles (600 kilometers) from Switzerland, and nearly 200 miles (300 kilometers) from the Baltic ports that led to neutral Sweden (see Figure 2.1). This location made any escape very arduous because of the distance that had to be covered.

The architects intentionally sited the prison in an area where the subsoil was bright yellow sand. The loose sand, they believed, would make tunneling nearly impossible. Also, it would be easy for the guards to pick up on digging activity if they noticed sand anywhere above ground.

Escape proof

The authorities cleared an area in the surrounding pine forest and initially laid out two compounds, one for officers and the other for enlisted men. In the officers' compound, barrack blocks (see Figure 2.2) were built and were set well apart and back from the perimeter fence. Double perimeter wire fences surrounded the camp (see Figure 2.3).

The most persistent POW escapees in the Allied Air Forces were held at Stalag Luft III, supposedly the most secure camp built expressly for the purpose of containing escape

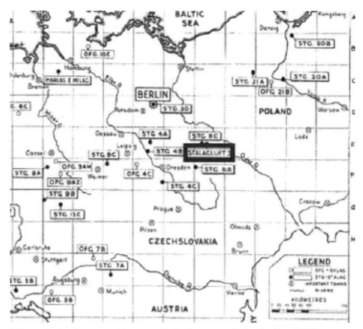

Figure 2.1: A geographic map of the location of Stalag Luft III.

artists. As a record, there were dozens of new security measures to make it escapeproof, including the following ones:

- Barrack blocks were built on pillars, in a bid to discourage tunneling, with only concrete foundations below the washrooms and stoves.

- A 10-foot (3-meter) double perimeter fence was topped with coils of barbed wire and a 7-foot (2 meter) space between each fence was also layered with more barbed wire.

- Microphones were buried beneath the camp's barbed-wire fences to pick up sounds of POWs digging their way out. As underground noises were detected, they triggered seismographs.

49

Figure 2.2: A barrack block built on pillars.

Figure 2.3: Double perimeter fence surrounding the camp.

- Watchtowers were situated at regular intervals along the perimeter fence and were permanently manned by guards with machine guns and spotlights. The POWs called their guards "goons," and the watchtowers were known as "goon boxes."

Figure 2.4: Watch and guard towers surrounded the camp.

- A low, knee-high, 18-inch (0.45 meter) warning wire, situated 30 feet (9 meters) in from the inner fence, ringed the inside of the camp's perimeter fence (see Figure 2.5) and sent a signal to the guards on contact. It marked the boundary of a no man's land that POWs were forbidden to cross without permission, and any prisoners caught beyond this line were liable to be shot by guards at the top of the watchtowers.

- Stalag Luft III's solitary confinement block, which POWs dubbed the "cooler," was a routine destination for any prisoner who broke the rules. The duration of a POW's stay depended on the whim of the guards, but any POW caught conspiring to escape could count on several weeks inside.

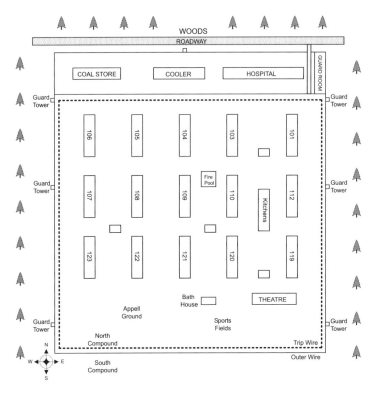

Figure 2.5: An aerial map of the camp or compound. The huts or barrack blocks each held 100 POWs and a double wire perimeter fence surrounded the camp.

The Opposing Team

The captors comprised members of the *Luftwaffe* (German Air Force) military structure. They viewed the POWs as fellow officers and treated them fairly well, despite an erratic and inconsistent supply of food. However, the German military's principal objective was to prevent escape, and this is where the line was drawn.

Kommandant

The prisoners were handled quite fairly within the guidelines of the Geneva Convention, and the Kommandant, *Oberst* (Colonel) Freidrich-Wilhelm von Lindeiner-Wildau, was a professional and honourable soldier who won the respect of the senior POWs.

Figure 2.6: Kommandant, Oberst (Colonel) Freidrich-Wilhelm von Lindeiner-Wildau.

Guards or Goons

The personnel of the prison camp changed frequently, and many of the guards were older or wounded combatants who had been on the Eastern Front. They had lost an arm or a leg or were incapacitated in some other fashion but were still able to perform guard duty. The guards were actually very astute at times. They had been guarding POWs long enough to know and anticipate many of the ways they would try to escape.

In some cases, these guards were fairly friendly. Some of them had emigrated to Canada or the United States before the war and had then returned to Germany when it seemed more prosperous. As a result, they were perfectly fluent in English.

Figure 2.7: Head Guard Glimnitz

Ferrets

These were German Army intelligence troops, anti-escape specialists with expertise in escape detection. They could enter the compound at any time and just wander around the camp, searching huts without warning.

Figure 2.8: Ferrets, escape specialists with expertise in escape detection.

Dog Handlers

These were guards who handled vicious German shepherd guard dogs. These dogs were used extensively to pick up on any suspicious scents, and they were brought into the camp each evening to sniff around before lights-out.

The Captured

These were the captives or prisoners of war, known as POWs or *Kriege*, from the German term for prisoner of war, Kriegsgefangener.

Figure 2.9: POW identification card issued to all POWs.

POWs

The camp housed mainly British and American airmen whose planes had crashed on Axis territory, but the 10,000 prisoners also included airmen of many other nationalities: French, Polish, Belgian, Dutch, Canadian, Australian, Lithuanian, Norwegian, New Zealander, South African, Greek, and Czechoslovakian. The Senior British Officer (SBO), Captain Massey, was seen as the principal leader and representative by both sides.

Duty

For the captured POWs, the words, "For you the war is over" were usually the first they heard. However, it was the sworn duty of all captured military personnel to continue to fight the enemy by surviving, communicating information, and escaping. Many viewed escape as an obligation and responsibility of airmen. Many of the POWs at Sagan were recaptured escapees, and for them it became a methodical struggle to escape starvation and regain their freedom. The guards believed that security at the new camp was so tight that it would be impossible for anyone to escape.

Motivation to Escape

The Geneva Convention of 1929 established guidelines for the humane treatment of POWs to ensure that they received as much protection as possible. Despite the general compliance with these principles, the inevitable reality for the captives in Stalag Luft III was still war, still prison, and still grim. After a long time in captivity, some POWs began to develop an obsession with the idea of escape. Many had been incarcerated for years and resented wasting the best years of their lives in confinement. These prisoners were also desperate to play their part in the war, having no idea how long the conflict could go on but believing that it could possibly continue for another five, ten, or twenty years.

For most POWs, escape was a sports field game where both sides knew the rules and there was a mutual respect between them. Some POWs saw escape as a way of life and the only means of preserving their sanity after years in a camp.

In fact, of all the POWs in the camp, fifty percent would help in an escape attempt, forty-five percent would like to escape, and five percent were determined to escape.

Living Conditions

Each hut was designed for one hundred men and was divided up into eighteen rooms measuring about 15 feet square (4.5 meters square). Every room had triple-decker bunks, stools, lockers, and a stove and served as a bedroom, dining room, and living room. There was a small room at the end of the hut allocated to a senior officer, like a wing commander. There was also a tiny kitchen with a coal stove (two burners and an oven) and a washroom.

Figure 2.10: Each room had triple-decker bunks and served as a bedroom, dining room, and living room.

Rations

Breakfast rations consisted of ersatz coffee made from acorns and dry black bread. Sauerkraut soup and a portion of mouldy potatoes followed for lunch, and dinner was some sausage or a peculiar cheese made from fish by-products. This was the standard diet for a non-working civilian, but at 800 calories per day it offered far less than the optimum 1,200 calories recommended for a normal healthy adult.

Figure 2.11: A worker filling a soup vat, a pressure cooker, where soup and bread were the main staples of the rations.

As the war continued, Allied bombing impacted the railroads and the already meager rations were cut in half. The food supply for the German people diminished along with the prison rations, and a lot of second-rate food, like turnips, ersatz sugar, and more ersatz coffee, started to appear.

Figure 2.12: Typical food rations for one POW for one week. Missing is the meat which sometimes went into the once-a-day soup issue.

As each room of the hut operated as a separate and self-sufficient mess hall, it was possible to prepare some extra food from the vegetable gardens, but overall there was very little to snack on. The problem of insufficient food rations was getting more desperate with time.

Figure 2.13: The content description of a Red Cross food parcel, broken down by nationality of the POWs, and a list of the weekly rations provided by the authorities.

Red Cross Parcels

Every week parcels arrived for the POWs, mostly from Britain, Canada, Australia, and the United States via the International Red Cross. Individual parcels were sent and paid for by relatives for a named person, and these parcels contained a mixture of goods. Bulk parcels for general distribution were also sent and paid for by the International Red Cross, and these contained a single supply of items that were pooled by the POWs. Thus, replacement clothing, shaving and washing kits, coffee, tea, tinned meat, jam, sugar, raisins, and other essentials were distributed equally (see Figure 2.14). The Red Cross also made routine inspection visits of the camps.

Figure 2.14: Typical foodstuffs that were found in a Red Cross parcel.

Isolation

No newspapers or radios were allowed in the camp, and the lack of news had a psychological impact. However, POWs resorted to using homemade sets. They continually disassembled the sets and hid their individual parts separately throughout the hut, so that discovery of one item did not compromise the whole set. These pieces were concealed in musical instruments or hut fixtures like light switches or fittings. Such precautions were essential because if the authorities discovered a complete set, the POWs responsible for it were liable to be shot.

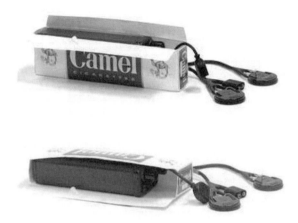

Figure 2.15: POWs homemade radio set hidden in a cigarette box.

Keeping Busy

The authorities thought that POWs who were kept happy, busy, and entertained would be less likely to escape, so the prisoners of Stalag Luft III enjoyed various privileges. Although heating and washing facilities were primitive, there was a well-stocked prison library that allowed POWs to study.

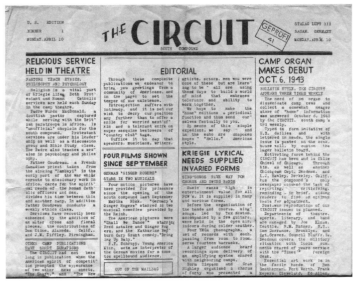

Figure 2.16: Newspaper edited and published by POWs.

Entertainment

The camp also had a 350-seat theatre that the POWs had built themselves, and this theatre allowed the prisoners to stage their own amateur dramatic productions. These theatrical performances served as a convenient subterfuge because the POWs could hire costumes from German theatre people and masquerade very effectively as women. The Kommandant supported the theatrical activities, being proud of the theatre and its impact on the POWs.

Figure 2.17: POWs took great pride in their theatrical productions, even renting costumes locally.

Education

The camp had a very active school that presented lectures every day. POWs could study any subjects they chose and could take exams in these areas from the Royal Society of Arts. Many POWs did much more than idly passing time in school activities. They took the opportunity to study for degrees and then passed their final exams, qualifying themselves for work in professions such as law and engineering. The papers were sent out by the Red Cross and invigilated through the University of London.

Exercise

POWs were encouraged to exercise and take part in sports in the summer and winter. The southern part of the camp had fields assigned for soccer, and volleyball in the summer, and ice hockey in the winter.

Figure 2.18: Exercise was encouraged through various sports like ice hockey in the winter.

Wire Happy

This was a term for POWs who were slowly going insane, a fate that could happen to any of them at some point or other after a period of incarceration.

Conclusions

Considering the hardships of capture and incarceration and the harsh conditions of the camp, it is almost unimaginable that POWs could organise themselves for an escape that involved any more than one or two escapees. So why would so many prisoners risk their lives by attempting to escape? After years in a camp, escape was a daily preoccupation offering hope and a hold on sanity for many POWs, yet they faced a hostile environment with authorities trying to shut down anything suspicious or too organised. Under these difficult conditions, with no resources or support, getting organised took a massive effort just to get over basic barriers confronting the captives. The fact that the prisoners were able to get any project off the ground, much less an escape plan of such scope and complexity, was simply incredible.

So how did the POWs get organised enough to surmount all the obstacles designed to make escape next to impossible? Any escape plans had to see beyond the multitude of problems to a clear objective, and to be so highly organised they needed tremendous leadership. Mental attitude was incredibly important, and the prevailing military discipline and the overall RAF rank structure helped to maintain both morale and authority.

In today's world it is likewise essential to a project's success to have an organised structure to work under and a code of discipline amongst the project people. This system supports team members and gives them the confidence to move forward, especially when the project is faced with a multitude of problems.

Although the guard-POW relationship seemed clear-cut on the surface, in reality it was much less straightforward, as both sides were trying to control and keep track of the other all the time. In fact, the relationship between captors and captives was very complex and polarised. For the POWs, relationships could appear to be very cosy as they established contacts, but typically this was only a superficial and exploitative means to gain something needed for the escape. For the guards, the type of relationship with the POWs could vary, depending on individual viewpoints. On the one hand, some guards were respectful of POWs and even sympathetic to their plight. In one situation, a guard was an anti-Nazi who went as far as providing documents and even contacting the French resistance for the prisoners.[6] On the other hand, there could be outright animosity between captors and captives, as guards were prepared to shoot escapers and the POWs always knew this. The guards were under tremendous pressure to toe the line and maintain strict control over the POWs.

CHAPTER THREE

Gathering the Requirements

"We've all dug tunnels in POW camps scattered all over Germany. In East Compound we dug, lost or abandoned at least fifty tunnels." Roger Bushell, Big X[5]

This chapter looks at gathering the requirements and understanding the complexities and interdependencies of the problems faced by the project. In any project, understanding the problems confronting it is an essential first step to creating a solution.

Problems of Escape

There were many problems facing the escape project, and their captors had deliberately set these up. Typically, the resolution of one problem only uncovered a further problem that was even more complex and more difficult, as shown in Figure 3.1.

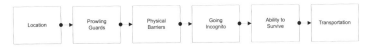

Figure 3.1: The many problems facing the project, where the resolution of one problem only uncovered a further problem that was even more complex and more difficult.

Location

The first problem preventing escape was the location of Stalag Luft III and the unknown outside world beyond it. Sagan was 100 miles (160 kilometers) southeast of Berlin, about as far as possible from the neutral Sweden, Switzerland, and Spain, so any escape was going to require a lot of travel and involve many elements. In 1943, getting around the Third Reich was difficult because of the constant stop-checks and searches by the police, military, and Gestapo. No persons could travel without documents detailing who they were, where they were traveling, and why.

Figure 3.2: Location of Stalag Luft III in the Third Reich.

Prowling Guards

The second problem preventing escape was keeping the
activities hidden from the prowling guards and ferrets. Their
constant surveillance forced the prisoners to carefully conceal
documents, equipment, clothing, and sand from the tunnels in
various hiding places. Ferrets, German Army intelligence
troops specialising in escape detection, could enter the
compound at any time and wander in and out of huts.
English-speaking ferrets lay under barracks listening to
conversations. Often, even after detection tunneling was
allowed to continue without intervention until near
completion, to keep the POWs busy and prevent them from
working on other escape plans.

Every second day after morning roll call or *appell,* about thirty ferrets and guards entered one block and threw everyone out. They then proceeded to search the hut from top to bottom for about three hours, leaving nothing unturned. They would search different huts each time and select them randomly. Sometimes they would take advantage of the empty block to hide in the ceiling whilst the POWs were outside on appell.

Figure 3.3: Roll call was called twice daily where all the POWs were counted.

Physical Barriers

The third problem preventing escape was the number of physical barriers around the camp. Search towers with floodlights, double barbed-wire fences, trip wires, and shoot zones surrounded Luft III. With any surface escape, there was a very high risk of being spotted.

To prevent tunnel escapes, the huts were set up off the ground on stilts, the fence was well over 100 yards (90 meters) from the huts, and microphones monitored by the administrative compound were placed every 33 feet (10 meters) to detect digging. With any tunnel, there was a very high risk that the tunnel would collapse and sand would come pouring down with little warning. Ventilation was a problem, and a means of getting enough air into the tunnel had to be devised. Without proper ventilation, men would vomit after a few hours of digging because of the foul air.

Figure 3.4: Position of the huts relative to the perimeter fence.

Traveling Incognito

The fourth problem preventing escape was the need to travel incognito in the outside world. This included mastering a certain level in a language and culture that were foreign to most British and Canadians and going unnoticed by wearing disguises.

The camp was hermetically sealed from surrounding communities, who were likely to be unfriendly to the POWs because they were airmen. The camp guards (who would recognise escaped prisoners) lived in the local towns and villages, so it was a problem just to get out unrecognised.

Ability to Survive

The fifth problem preventing escape was the issue of surviving in a harsh environment and climate. In the winter and spring, the night temperatures were well below freezing, and from December to April heavy snow lay on the ground, so the summer was escape season. The POWs would have very limited access to water and food and would have to carry most of these necessities on their persons.

Transportation

The sixth problem preventing escape was the access to transportation to get to a neutral country and safety. If the POWs could secure transport, they could get away from the camp and the search cordons. Methods of transport included trains (passenger and goods), bicycles, and boats/ships. One advantage that they had was the proximity of the local train station at Sagan, less than 1 mile (1.6 kilometers) away.

Reasons to Attempt Escape

For some POWs there was little reason to attempt escape, and they accepted their uncertain fates, but for others the drive and determination were almost overwhelming. Apart from a sense of duty that compelled them to escape, POWs felt the helplessness of having no control over their own lives and existing within an extremely confined environment. Life was unbearably boring. Escape provided excitement, purpose, and hope, while the monotony of imprisonment would last an indefinite length of time.

Escape was a restless itch for about twenty-five percent of the camp population, and only five percent of those were considered to be dedicated escapers. The others would, however, work in support of any escape attempts.

Ways Out

There were three ways out of any camp: under, over, or through the wire. Tunnels were the main way under a prison, although in camps such as Colditz, housed in a castle on a high hill, there was little hope of deep, underground tunneling.

Getting out over the wire or wall was very risky as it was the most highly visible escape and it inevitably took place high up, away from the cover of any shadows.

Going through any barriers could take the form of either a direct assault, like wire cutting, or a subterfuge, such as hiding in carts or wagons brought into the camp or wearing a disguise and pretending to be someone with a legitimate reason for leaving. The latter tactic tended to be opportunistic, and the escapers had to be extensively agile and adept at sensing the potential for escape and responding in time before the chance disappeared.

Previous Attempts

In Stalag Luft III, there were many escape attempts throughout the history of the camp, to the point where the authorities set up a museum to house the escape equipment, artifacts, and photos of the tunnels. The museum was used to train new guards and to impress upon visitors the lengths to which POWs were capable of going. In one escape attempt, a POW who was dressed as a ferret walked out of the camp at night. Another prisoner hid in a truck that brought in food. During a routine inspection by the Red Cross Commission, a group of POWs walked out in civilian clothes, pretending to be part of the commission. One prisoner walked out dressed as a sweeper whilst the real sweeper was still inside.

In one of the most audacious escape attempts, two POWs found a blind spot they believed to be hidden from sight of two guard towers. A diversion was created by hundreds of men who attracted the attention of guards in four of the towers by staging a "sham" fight, calling for permission to collect a ball, and so on. In the meantime, the two escapers crossed to the fence and carefully cut through the strands of wire so they could get out to the wooded area outside. Eventually they were caught and returned, but typically most attempts failed and resulted in the punishment of fourteen days of solitary confinement in the cooler.

Odds of Getting Out

Escaping required a lot of preparation, and the odds of making a "home run" out of Germany during an escape were very small, about 28 to 1 against success. Out of 10,000 RAF POWs, only 30 succeeded in reaching home, so to increase the odds for success, POWs relied on escape aids, forgery, and disguises.

Conclusions

In gathering the requirements, the first step is to clearly define and articulate the problems, the pain associated with these, and the value or gain in solving these. The risks to the prisoners were very high, but it was possible to escape. There were two approaches to escape: an ad hoc method or a well planned, extremely detailed one. After two or three years of incarceration and extensive escape experience, the POWs became very familiar with the obstacles facing any escape attempt. With either an improvised or well-prepared approach, prisoners had to find a solution to each one of these problems. There were often several solutions to a problem, and over time one superior solution would emerge as the best.

Similarly, in today's world the detection of the best solution whilst working in a project may take several evolutions, but typically the most important factor is understanding the problems at a level of enough detail.

CHAPTER FOUR

Project Initiation

"In North Compound we are concentrating our efforts on completing and escaping through one master tunnel. No private-enterprise tunnels allowed. Three bloody deep, bloody long tunnels will be dug – Tom, Dick, and Harry. One will succeed." Roger Bushell, Big X[5]

In today's world, projects follow various life cycles. In this story of escape, the closest life cycle is listed with four phases:

1. Initiation

2. Planning and Design

3. Construction

4. Implementation and Breakout

This chapter reviews how the project was initiated and the project team was brought together to plan the project. This requires the careful selection of team members to form a core team.

In today's projects, each project phase is completed by the delivery of one or more deliverables. The PMBOK™[7] advocates not only phases and deliverables but also knowledge areas that need to be fulfilled through the course of the project (see Table 4.1 below).

Table 4.1: The nine knowledge areas are essential to a project as advocated by the *Guide to the Project Management Body of Knowledge.*

Knowledge Areas	*Description*
Integration Management	Integrates all eight knowledge areas and includes project plan development, integrated change control, and project execution
Scope Management	Plans and defines the scope, identifies major deliverables and the work breakdown structure (WBS), and does the organisation's cost-benefit analysis
Time Management	Defines the activities in the project, completes the activity sequencing, and develops the schedule
Cost Management	Defines estimates, develops a budget, and controls cost

Quality Management	Plans the approach to quality in a project, identifies the required quality characteristics, and builds the quality assignments into the schedule
Human Resource Management	Manages the stakeholders and the team throughout the lifecycle, identifies skill requirements for assignments, and sets team development and rewards
Communications Management	Determines stakeholders, plans communications, sets expectations, distributes information, reports performance, and manages stakeholders
Risk Management	Makes initial assumptions that affect the project, develops the risk management plan, identifies and analyses risk, and plans response and implementation of the risk and contingency plans
Procurement Management	Plans and solicits bids, assesses make-or-buy decisions, and negotiates contract, administration, and closeout

The following four chapters of the book are structured around these nine knowledge areas, and although these areas were not generally articulated in 1943, the escape committee members intuitively followed them within their project life cycle.

Escape Committee

Through trial and error, and many thwarted escape attempts, it was realised early on that for any escape attempt to succeed it had to be well planned and well organised. The POWs at Sagan therefore established a highly organised escape committee, known as the "X Organisation," to oversee any escape attempts. The escape committee existed in many camps and its primary role was to accept proposals for escape plans. Any applicant whose proposal was approved could choose his own team and proceed forward with the plan. The escape committee also schemed its own plans, and each member had to play a specific role and run a certain department.

Leadership of Escape Committee

The elected leader of the escape committee was Squadron Leader Roger Bushell, or "Big X" (see Figure 4.1). He was selected as the CEO (Chief Escape Officer) because he was a natural leader and had quite a reputation for escaping from various camps. He had been sent to Stalag Luft III because it was built with great care and planning and considered escapeproof by the authorities.

Bushell developed his reputation at a previous camp, Dulag Luft, where he was appointed the escape committee's chief of intelligence and became one of the most relentless escapers of all Allied POWs.

Bushell was actually a student in Germany before the war. He was from South Africa, so he spoke Boer, and he was quite fluent in German. He was a vigorous all-rounder who shone academically but was also a tireless partygoer and a good enough skier to represent his university. His attitude on skiing mirrored his attitude on life, which he approached with a fearlessness that bordered on recklessness. His success lay in his ability to calculate the degree of risk and take that to the limit.

Figure 4.1: Squadron Leader Roger Bushell, leader of the escape committee, or "Big X."

Before the war, Bushell gained a reputation as a defense lawyer, while his love of speed inevitably drew him to flying, and in 1932 he joined 601 Squadron of the Royal Auxiliary Air Force, a squadron of young elite men known as "The Millionaires' Club." Anton Gill notes, "His character contained precisely the correct mixture of arrogance, intelligence, patriotism and daring to form him for action."[8]

In the spring of 1941, after hiding in a shed on the edge of the exercise field, Bushell escaped as far as the Swiss border, posing as a ski instructor, before being caught. In another escape attempt, he and three others, whilst in transit between camps, escaped through the floor of a train wagon via a hole they had cut with a stolen table knife. Bushell was eventually recaptured in Prague.

Bushell's Approach as Project Manager

Bushell was a good listener and gave everyone an opportunity to participate. For example, when anyone came up with a plausible escape plan, he would listen to it, criticise the plan, and then approve or disapprove it.

Bushell as a project manager ran a very tight ship, and his word was pretty much law. He had a mind like a filing cabinet and was very good at organising. He got a great deal of respect from the POWs and at the same time from the guards as well. His captors readily acknowledged that he was a dangerous individual, so he was watched in particular. He was very careful about his activities so he would not give away that he was up to something. Bushell had been officially warned that if he tried to escape again, he would be shot. He disguised his activities by spending his spare time working with languages, teaching German and learning Czech, Danish, and Russian.

Throughout the project, Bushell did not usually get involved in technical arguments, leaving those to individual chiefs to resolve. If he did intercede, it was to settle a dispute that had escalated to the point of causing discontent, and he would settle it very quickly.

Previous Experiences

The escape committee had experienced the consequences of having an escape plot discovered prematurely by the camp authorities. The event was devastating to the escapers, specifically when a tunnel was involved. In the East Compound they had lost or abandoned at least fifty tunnels in a thirty-month time frame. Men had toiled for months, only to see their efforts leading to nothing, so they were used to project failure and the demoralising effects of it. Bushell recognised from these failures that everything hinged on security.

Switching Compounds

In March of 1943 a new North Compound was created at Sagan to relieve some of the overcrowding. The SBO approached the Kommandant and suggested that a few POW working parties help in the building of the new compound. The Kommandant, believing the offer was in the right spirit of cooperation and likely to raise morale, unknowingly introduced members of the escape committee into the compound. They paced and mapped the layout of the camp, calculated distances and angles, and surveyed the area outside of the wire. They began to put together all the details for the escape, such as where to dig the tunnels and how long they should be. One of the German surveyors handed over the plans for the compound, and the POWs stole them and carried them back to be studied. These diagrams revealed the underground sewage system and two tunnels leading out to nearby drainage areas.

Figure 4.2: The Kommandant unknowingly introduced members of the escape committee into the new compound.

In April the first guards shepherded the 850 POWs from Stalag Luft III's overcrowded East Compound into the newly built North Compound. The prisoners carried all their worldly possessions and were searched, but nothing was found. With them went the intact X Organisation that had overseen escapes there. The move to the North Compound presented an opportunity for the POWs, who profited by the confusion caused by taking up their brand-new quarters and started plotting an escape. The SBO pledged that both he and the entire camp were committed to Bushell and his escape plans. Unfortunately, the sewer tunnels they had seen on the compound plans proved to be too narrow for escape.

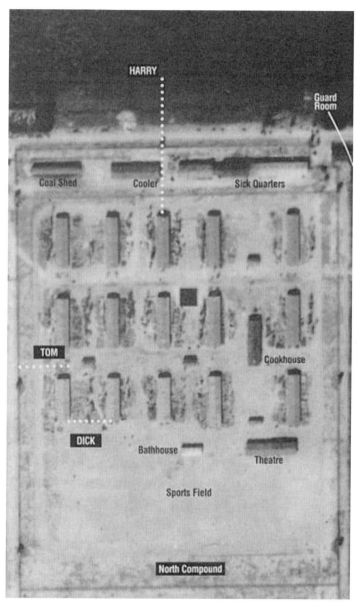

Figure 4.3: Ariel photo of the new North Compound for the Allied POWs.

Integration Management

This knowledge area (see Table 4.1) covers the integration of all of the knowledge areas. Early in the project, it includes project plan development.

Developing a Project Charter

Bushell and the escape committee were faced with the conundrum of determining the best possible approach to escape, and this varied depending on the available resources and the overall risk to the camp, as shown in Table 4.2 below. By analysing the resources and risks, they could determine the best Return on Investment (ROI).

Bushell had been planning to implement an idea since March, in line with the final option in Table 4.2, which was not so much to return escapers to the United Kingdom but to cause a giant internal problem for the German administration.

Bushell declared to the escape committee, "Everyone here in this room is living on borrowed time. By rights we should all be dead! The only reason that God allowed us this extra ration of life is so we can make life hell for the Hun . . . In North Compound we are concentrating our efforts on completing and escaping through one master tunnel. No private-enterprise tunnels allowed. Three bloody deep, bloody long tunnels will be dug: Tom, Dick, and Harry. One will succeed!"[9]

The escape committee chose to go with Bushell's recommendation. Even though it was the riskiest plan, the escape committee was compelled to try it based on experience and the possibility of getting many POWs out.

Table 4.2: Determining the escape approach based on resources and risks.

Approach: Unplanned, opportunistic - take advantage of a presented situation

Example	# Escapees	Resources Required	Risk
Hide in the back of a truck	1-2	Low	Low

Approach: Planned, used once only - escape route exposed

Example	# Escapees	Resources Required	Risk
Cutting through wire	1-3	Medium	Low

Approach: Planned, reused several times - escape route preserved; goal is a mass escape over a long period

Example	# Escapees	Resources Required	Risk
Tunnel	1-10	Medium	High

Approach: Planned, used once only - escape route exposed

Example	# Escapees	Resources Required	Risk
Deep tunnel	Up to 250	High	High

> *"He [Bushell] decreed that there were to be only three tunnels, Tom, Dick and Harry, and they were to be all built simultaneously on identical lines. No other tunneling was to be allowed because previously we had all been burrowing like bunnies all over the place,"* Jimmy James told BBC Radio Shropshire in an interview in 2000.[10]

The overall project objectives were complex, but the escape committee reached a clear consensus at the outset about the desired outcome of the project. In short, it was to give escapers an opportunity to get to a neutral country and back into the war, although the odds of success varied with each POW. The project was tangible, had an intrinsic value, and included a charter that could be described in some detail at the start of the project.

Developing a Preliminary Project Scope Statement

Many elements that defined the scope of the escape project had to be carefully considered. For example:

- Number of tunnels dug, determined by the number of concrete foundations available and the risk of discovery

- Depth and length of the tunnels, determined by the distance from the camp to the woods and available tunnel shoring materials

- Scope of intelligence and security required, as at any time six guards were wandering around in the compound

- Number of escapers that could get through a tunnel in a given night

The preliminary scope was mainly based on the available resources, and Bushell's demands for the project were high. He asked the escape committee for various project deliverables: 200 passes to be forged, 200 civilian suits, 200 compasses, and 1000 maps, for instance.

Conclusions

In project initiation, the first step is to get buy-in for making an investment of resources in the project and then assign a project manager to lead the project. The project manager then forms his team and starts preparing plans. The single reason that most projects fail is the lack of planning. With the Great Escape, project planning was done by a very experienced team that inherently understood the problems and the risks. Through many previous failed escape attempts, they could analyse where things had gone wrong and mitigate these factors for the current project. They were also better able to assess the risks that were constantly changing.

Likewise, in today's world there are many past lessons that can be applied to present-day projects. Most notable is the ability to accurately assess the risk based on the understanding of the problem and the previous experience of failed projects.

The escape committee (project team) came to the compound with the right background and mindset. They were either experts in a specific area or the most experienced in a required activity. Even before the camp was built, they already had it staked out and had plans in place for the escape. They carried the scars of previous unsuccessful escapes and knew the massive obstacles that lay ahead of them. This track record of failure made them more determined to come together and work as a project team.

The lynchpin in the project team was Roger Bushell, and he did not have to do a lot of selling to persuade this group to work closely together for a common cause. Bushell brought a mental toughness to the project, and he could see beyond the immediate obstacles and multitude of problems to a clear objective. Bushell also brought tremendous organisational ability to the table and knew precisely what activities had to be undertaken. He was a natural leader to whom POWs turned, and this was important because the lack of resources meant that most of the POWs had to get behind the project and its single cause. The next chapter will look at how the project took shape through the planning phase.

CHAPTER FIVE

Planning and Design

"The Germans might—rephrase that—probably will discover Tom, Dick, or Harry, because over the past few years they've become as clever at finding tunnels as we have at building them. But three deep and technologically expert tunnels should give us an edge . . . From now on every one of us here has got to think not what the Germans think, but to get one step ahead of that thinking." Roger Bushell, Big X[5]

This chapter looks at how the project team starts to plan the project and work through the high-level design of the solution. This requires viewing the project through nine knowledge areas.

Integration Management

This knowledge area (see Table 4.1) covers the integration of all the knowledge areas and includes project plan development, integrated change control, and project execution.

Developing a Project Management Plan

Bushell was involved in every detail of the project planning. Although no physical plan was ever produced, this is what the plan might have looked like based on the activities that took place:

- Initiation
    - Idea, Approach, Proposal, ROI
    - Checkpoint 1: Escape Committee— Assess Risk, Designate Resources
- Planning and Design
    - High-Level Plan, Blueprint
    - Checkpoint 2: Escape Committee— Assess Risk, Apply Resources
- Construction
    - Preparation of Tunnel
    - Engineering of Tunnel
    - Construction and Testing
    - Preparation for Escape
    - Checkpoint 3: Escape Committee— Assess Risk to Determine Likelihood of Success

- Implementation and Breakout

  – Implement Escape

  – Checkpoint 4: Escape Committee—
    Assess Risk to Determine Likelihood of
    Success

  – Collect Metrics and Determine Success

  – Consider Rerun (Reuse)

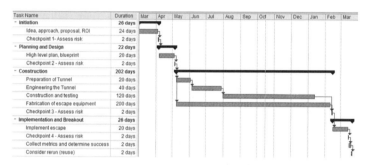

Figure 5.1: Gantt chart of the Great Escape.

Creating a WBS (Work Breakdown Structure)

This activity builds the Work Plan and Budget. For the escape
project, this included the major project deliverables like the
tunnel and all the paraphernalia or escape aids required for an
escape, such as clothing, equipment, documents, and so forth.

Time Management

This knowledge area (see Table 4.1) defines the activities in the project, completes the activity sequencing, and develops the schedule.

In the Great Escape project this was a very important factor, as the shorter the timeline, the less likely the escape plot would be discovered. Therefore, a shorter construction time meant a lower risk.

Activity Definition

The escape committee defined the principal activities as:

- Tunnel Engineering

- Sand Removal and Dispersal

- Construction of Escape Aids (this activity could continue in parallel without any dependencies on the previous two activities)

Activity Sequencing

The following activities were closely dependent:

- Tunnel Engineering

- Sand Removal and Dispersal

The latter impacted the former as the rate of sand removal and dispersal dictated the rate of tunnel engineering.

Activity Resource Estimating

This was determined based on previous experience and a number of local conditions such as soil composition, climate, and the ability to disperse sand. The type of structure was also important, and tunnel engineering required a very skilled team, specific engineering tools (spades), and materials to shore up the tunnel.

Activity Duration Estimating

This determination was based on previous experience. For example, soil structure dictated the rate of digging, and this was on the project's critical path. Closely correlated to this was the rate of removal and dispersal of sand as well as various conditions that impacted this rate. The ferrets were constantly looking for traces of the easily distinguishable sand.

Schedule Development

The climate dictated a tunneling season during the spring and summer, and with the move to the new camp scheduled for April, the tunneling had to begin right away.

Cost Management

This knowledge area (see Table 4.1) defines estimates, develops a budget, and controls cost.

Cost Estimating

Cost was measured in human labour and not by a monetary value. One of the assets of the escape project was the availability of human labour and the prisoners' willingness to work, although it would be unfair to say there was no cost to it. As in all projects, "incentives" were required to drive the project, and these were found in a number of ways:

- Extra rations

- Escape privileges, like priority in the escape queue

Cost Budgeting

Red Cross parcels were carefully managed and used as a currency to procure goods from the guards (see "Procurement Management"), or these goods could be traded for local currency. Food, a precious resource, was also used to motivate the POWs. Although escape was a motivation in itself, there were periods when morale could drop considerably. Raisins and sugar were used to distill "raisin wine," a highly potent alcoholic beverage reserved for special occasions to raise morale.

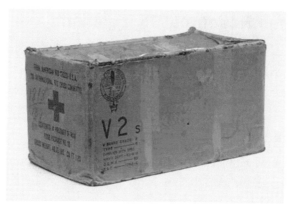

Figure 5.2: A red cross parcel used as a currency through the camp.

Quality Management

This knowledge area (see Table 4.1) plans the approach to quality in a project, identifies the required quality characteristics, and builds the quality assignments into the schedule.

Quality Planning

Clearly defining the quality goals of the project in the Quality Management Plan ensures that quality activities are planned, resources are assigned, and commitments are agreed to. Quality was important to the escape project and had to be considered in everything from the rigour of the escape route engineering through to the escape aids, clothing, and documents that would all come under very close scrutiny.

Human Resource Management

This knowledge area (see Table 4.1) manages the stakeholders and the team throughout the life cycle. It identifies skill requirements for assignments, team development, and rewards.

Human Resource Planning

This knowledge area clearly defines the project level structure and the work within the context of the organisational structure.

There were many professions, trades, and skills represented within the camp, including those of miners, forgers, tailors, carpenters, engineers, physicists, geologists, and surveillance experts. The escape committee had to match their skill sets against project activities to maximise the overall work effort.

Acquiring the Project Team

Intuitively Bushell knew what work had to be completed and the functions required to make the project a success:

- Internal Security

- Tunnel Engineering

- Escape Equipment and Toolmaking

- Intelligence Gathering

- Document Production

- Compass Factory

- Clothing Production

- Mapmaking

- Dispersal Diversion

- Supplies

- Dispersal

Bushell selected his departmental chiefs (project leaders) early on to give direction to the project (see Figure 5.3).

- Conk Canton, Adjutant (Military Assistant)

- Bud Junior Clark, Security Chief or Big S

- Wally Floody, Chief Engineer of Tunneling

- Johnny Travis, Escape Equipment Production Chief

- Wally Valenta, Intelligence Chief

- Tim Walenn (ex-artist), Document Production Chief

- Al Hake, Compass Factory Chief

- Tommy Guest (ex-tailor), Clothing Chief

- Des Plunkett, Mapmaking Chief

- Jerry Sage, Dispersal Diversion Chief

- Willy William, Supplies Chief

- Peter Hornblower, Dispersal Chief

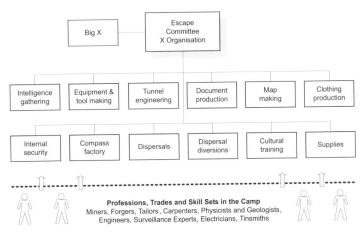

Figure 5.3: Organisational chart of the X Organisation showing its departmental chiefs (project leaders).

With the departmental chiefs, the escape committee created project teams for each department to overcome the various problems that were allocated to these teams, based on the available skill sets.

Developing the Project Team

Practically everyone in the camp was involved in some capacity with the escape project, so there was a massive pool of skill sets for the respective teams. Some skills could be readily used, but others were less obvious. For instance, carpenters from the camp theatre would be employed in constructing the wooden supports to shore up the tunnel.

Tailors who were very skilled in sewing would convert uniforms into either civilian clothes or German-looking uniforms. Electricians would link the tunnels to the camp

Figure 5.4: Carpenters from the camp theatre would be employed in the tunnel.

electrical supply for lighting. Tinsmiths would convert empty dried-milk tins into the air trunks that ventilated the narrow tunnels. Forgers would prepare false documents for use in moving about in Germany after the break.

Managing the Project Team

Few escape committees were so well integrated, so unselfish, or so single-minded in purpose. Bushell set the POWs to work creating everything needed to mount a massive escape, and he met his department chiefs every day to review the project and assess how much progress was made.

Bushell set up in each block (hut) a Little X and a Little S. Their role was to ensure that all prisoners were

103

screened for their skill sets to determine where they could fit into the project. With this set-up, there was a true matrix organisation (departments vertically and Little Xs horizontally).

Communications Management

This knowledge area (see Table 4.1) determines stakeholders, plans communications, sets expectations, distributes information, reports performance, and manages stakeholders.

Communications Planning

The escape committee communicated the plan to other POWs to get buy-in and active participation in the project. They had to unify the camp to work on this one project and dissuade POWs from working on other escape attempts that could compromise the Great Escape. The following factors were involved:

- Creation of compliance, adoption, and communication plans. The adoption plan was required to persuade the camp to:
  - Contribute resources to the project
  - Support the project
- Establishment and maintenance of high level of trust necessary for project success

Information Distribution

Everything was done through word of mouth. Little was ever written down, and if it was, it was on scraps of paper that were held by individuals and not shared.

Performance Reporting

Daily meetings of the escape committee reported the status and performance of their individual departments. Without a single Gantt chart, the teams were able to track progress of the project intuitively.

Managing Stakeholders

The POWs were also the principal stakeholders in the project. The expectation of most of them was that by participating in a mass breakout, a few prisoners would actually reach neutral territory. The majority of POWs wanted to tie down as many Axis forces as possible in extensive search efforts, and they expected to enjoy a few days of freedom before being recaptured.

One key player, Wally Floody, had rather more short-term expectations. He wanted to get out because he knew he would be recaptured and put in the cooler for two weeks. As the head of tunneling operations, Floody was overworked and exhausted, so the break would have been welcome. Bushell had to put a stop to this scheme.

One very important task was to coach new POWs not to react to unusual events to prevent them from alerting the guards to them. As Roger Bushell himself put it to a group of new arrivals, *"If you see me walking around with a tree trunk sticking out of my arse, don't ask any questions, because it'll be for a damned good reason."*

105

Risk Management

This knowledge area (see Table 4.1) makes initial assumptions that affect the project, develops the risk management plan, identifies and analyses risk, and plans response and implementation of the risk and contingency plans.

Risk Management Planning

This was critical, as there were many risks to the project, including discovery of the escape plot, dangerous work in the project, and escaping itself. The intricacies of these risks had to be identified and managed through carefully thought-out mitigation plans.

Risk Identification

This was based on keeping track of metrics related to escape attempts and going through a postmortem after each attempt, regardless of whether it failed or was successful.

The first area of risk was escape plot discovery. The shorter the timeline, the less likely it was that the escape plot would be discovered. The principal risk for the escape committee lay in the detection of the escape project through:

- Traces of the tunnel exposed or poorly hidden
- Nosy ferrets uncovering something

The second area of risk involved the dangers of tunnel engineering, hazardous work where men were risking their lives due to potential risks in:

- Tunnel construction and collapse

- Accumulation of bad air in tunnels

Risk analysis can be both qualitative and quantitative. The former (qualitatively) performs an analysis of the risks and conditions to prioritise their effects on project objectives. The latter (quantitatively) measures the probability and consequences of risks and estimates their implications for project objectives.

Qualitative Risk Analysis

With this risk analysis, two questions need to be answered:

- What is the probability of the event occurring?

- If the event occurs, what will be its impact?

For the first risk, escape plot discovery:

- The greatest risk concerned the tunnel itself. The probability of finding a deep tunnel was greatest in respect to its trap door, and the impact of the detection of an access trap was catastrophic. With only one entrance, it was critical to make sure the trap door to the tunnel entrance was well concealed.

- Nosy ferrets were also a very high risk, and they could wander anywhere and uncover something. The impact of this was that all escape-related work had to be closely guarded and POWs had to be alerted to the ferrets' presence.

- A slightly lesser risk was ineffectively hiding traces of the tunnel, particularly the sand. The impact of discovering sand was that the ferrets would be alerted to tunneling activity. This would increase the ferocity of the searches but would not reveal the tunnel's exact whereabouts.

For the second risk, dangers with tunnel engineering:

- The greatest risk was a tunnel collapse, which could happen suddenly with little warning, and its impact was injury and sometimes death.

- A lesser risk was with bad air saturated in carbon dioxide, and its impact was injury or even death.

Quantitative Risk Analysis

This calculates the cost of impact for each risk, in priority order of risks. So if the risk were to happen, what is the estimated cost in terms of effort, materials, equipment, and tools through direct and indirect costs (to other tasks)?

For the first risk, escape plot discovery:

- The cost of trap or tunnel discovery was almost catastrophic in that the costs were extremely high in terms of effort put in, thousands of man-hours, and quantity of shoring materials. Once a tunnel was detected, none of these would be recovered.

- The cost of not containing nosy ferrets could be measured in the loss of output of clandestine activities measured in effort put in, hundreds of man-hours, and the materials for the activity.

- The cost of tunnel sand discovery was very serious as it would likely increase the intensity of searches for the tunnel and hence put the project at risk.

For the second risk, dangers with tunnel engineering:

- The cost of collapsing tunnels was disastrous and could be measured in terms of lost lives.

- The cost of bad air saturated in carbon dioxide could also be measured in terms of serious injury or loss of lives.

Risk Response Planning

The approach is to reduce the likelihood or impact of the event by taking risk response strategies, as for example:

1. Transfer the risk

2. Avoid the risk

3. Mitigate the risk

4. Accept the risk

Each department was responsible for managing the risks associated with its activities by employing risk management strategies.

For the first risk, escape plot discovery, the following strategies were employed:

- A major risk was discovery of the trap doors, and by paying great attention to their concealment this risk was lessened. Weeks were spent in designing these trap doors in such a way that they blended into the surroundings of the room.

- Ferrets expected tunneling to be ongoing, so contingency plans were drawn up in case one of the tunnels was discovered. Multiple tunnels were built in parallel in an effort to have a fallback route in case one was found.

- Some wire escape jobs, accomplished by breaking through the wire, were encouraged so as to leave the impression that escape attempts were still being carried out. It would look strange if all escape attempts suddenly stopped.

- By putting many resources into cover-up activities like diversion and sand dispersal, risk was mitigated in concealing traces of the tunnel.

- Nosy ferrets were a constant risk that was reduced through a system of tracking, and Bushell kept a list of ferrets that were deemed dangerous to the project.

- Another risk avoidance strategy was reading enemy intent, and this was done by continually monitoring what ferrets were thinking through contacts with friendly ferrets and reading between the lines.

For the second risk, dangers with tunnel engineering, the following strategies were employed:

- To lessen the risk of tunnel collapse, pains were taken to ensure that the tunnels were level. Any movement in an uneven tunnel could catch the supports or shoring and cause a collapse.

- Tunnelers had to devise a system to ensure that tunnels ended up where planned, pointing in the right direction and built at a level depth.

- Everyday tunnel engineering would mitigate risk by allowing continual careful scrutiny of the tunnel for signs of danger and potential tunnel collapse.

- A ventilation system was installed to bring air right up the tunnel face.

Procurement Management

This knowledge area (see Table 4.1) plans and solicits bids, assesses make-or-buy decisions, and negotiates contracts, administration, and closeout.

The escape committee procured resources like tools and raw materials essential to the project by either "liberating" (stealing) them or bribing the guards.

Planning Purchases and Acquisitions

Certain goods and products could not be produced internally, so the escape committee had to plan these purchases externally. Sometimes these necessary items could be liberated if the opportunity arose, but for the most part they had to be bought. Foodstuffs and tobacco from Red Cross parcels were used to acquire goods from the guards.

Bushell and the department chiefs had to work out what would have to be purchased versus what they would try to produce in the camp. For instance, one of the most difficult items to produce, and one that was important to the plot, was a camera.

Plan Contracting

Which guards would be approached and how? What was being purchased? What were the risks involved? All this had to be carefully planned out, and the department of supplies was part of this activity.

Requesting Seller Responses

Bushell's team of buyers had to work hard at "softening up" the guards to ensure they were going to fulfill the requests for needed goods.

Selecting Sellers

Bushell's team of buyers had to target pliable guards/ferrets (the sellers) who were corrupt and could be bribed or blackmailed. The POWs succeeded in procuring cameras through blackmail and a ruse of recording theatre productions.

Contract Administration

Bushell was ultimately responsible for interfacing between the buyers who had the relationships with the friendly guards/ferrets (the sellers) and the department chiefs who needed the purchases. He would administer the purchases and provide resources to ensure transactions were completed.

Contract Closure

As the escape project reached its latter stages, Bushell had to ensure that the ferrets would stay quiet about any items they had sold to the POWs. The guards were well aware that their positions were at risk if they were caught helping POWs.

Blueprint and High-Level Design of the Solution

In this project, the solutions were created from many components, and these stretched across each of the functions or departments of the X Organisation (see Figure 5.3). Each component would have a specific design. In the overall project, one of the most critical functions for the design was tunnel engineering.

Blueprint

This is a plan that documents an architectural or engineering design. It may take the form of a simple sketch, but traditionally it is produced by the contact printing process of the cyanotype, with the familiar white lines on a blue background. For the escape project, one blueprint would have shown the location of tunnels (see Figure 5.4). Other departments would have had blueprints for engineering components like the in-tunnel railway, air pumps, and so on.

Design of the Tunnel

The tunnel was the best solution to many of the physical barriers within and around the camp, such as the wire fences and guard towers. The tunnels were modeled after one that a POW saw in a smuggled magazine. The design (see Figure 5.5) was based on the huge bank of collective experience of the escape committee. For example, they realised they would have to go deep below the microphones and they considered the possibility that their captors would prod the ground with rods.

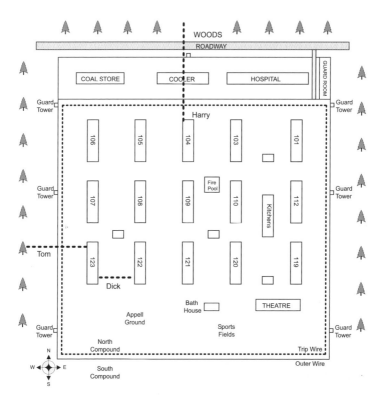

Figure 5.4: Blueprint of the location of the tunnels running from the camp.

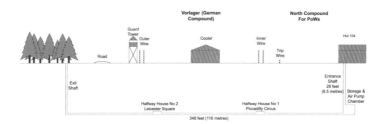

Figure 5.5: Design of the tunnel showing its planned depths and lengths.

Conclusions

In project planning and design, the first step is to go through the nine knowledge areas and initiate them: for example, the risk management processes, communications management, and so forth. These areas are fundamental to the success of a project. For the Great Escape, the success hinged completely on planning and design, as without these phases it would fail. Even though plans were never written down, the project was executed successfully, and this is a testament to the effectiveness of these plans.

In addition, any project should follow the nine knowledge areas intuitively, and this chapter showed how the Great Escape project mapped against these areas. For instance, one very important knowledge area concerned teamwork and hence the Human Resourcing for the project. Another was Risk Management, and with the project under constant threat the escape committee was continuously challenged, and this became an essential requirement. A third critical knowledge area was Quality Management where certain deliverables had to be nearly perfect, like documents, clothing, and the escape tunnel itself. Finally, Integration Management needs a mention as it pulled all the knowledge areas together.

CHAPTER SIX

Constructing Solutions to Problems

"Of course, being American, I was soon into the mass-production, Ford-assembly-line philosophy. Why not magnetize 20 razor blades at the same time? I took a flat bed board, used powdered skim milk to make a glue, and secured all the blades. I used the same stroking technique and increased production overnight." Al Hake, Compass Factory Chief

This chapter looks at the heart of the project, the construction phase, and this is where the construction begins. This phase created the solutions to the immediate problems that the escape committee faced. For example, one of the first steps was to initiate the creation of tunnel entrances. These became the cleverly concealed trap doors to the tunnels that were dug soon after.

Daily Project Meetings

Bushell met his departmental chiefs daily and listened to their problems, made suggestions, and thrashed out decisions with them. He always supported the chiefs in carrying these out.

Intelligence Branch

This was a critical department, as whatever intelligence was gathered impacted other departments. Wally Valenta trained men who spoke German in the art of espionage. A "Duty Pilot" system consisted of a rota of officers that logged every guard or ferret entering the compound and tailed each of them everywhere.

In today's projects this department is often overlooked, and yet good intelligence can make or break a project.

Duty Pilots

These POWs sat by the gate with their runners, watching all the traffic entering and exiting the camp, noting time in and out, and keeping track of ferrets. Each duty pilot had a runner to send out to warn the stooges in the blocks to pick up ferrets.

Contacts

A POW "contact" was a German speaker assigned to befriend a ferret or administrator coming into the camp. The contact would soften up the target by offering him a brew, biscuits, or cigarettes, and the target ferret would find a sympathetic audience in the block. The contacts cultivated the friendship of individual guards and made them amenable to the point where they would bring contraband articles into camp in exchange for chocolate and cigarettes. Bribery usually worked with other goods like coffee, sugar, raisins, and soap, as these had not been widely available in Germany and were highly sought by the guards.

Usually the first bribe was the most difficult, as the targets wrestled with their consciences, but after that it became habitual and the guards proved cooperative, supplying railway timetables, maps, and official papers required for travel.

In a short time, the intelligence branch pooled information from all its contacts to build a big-picture view of life outside of the camp. The intelligence data included the geography of the surrounding area, timetables of outgoing trains, information on ticket prices, the location of Swedish ships in Stettin and Danzig, and details on the placement of guards covering the Swiss and Danish borders.

As the contacts became more confident, the requests became more audacious. One guard was blackmailed into bringing in a camera and film. Another ferret was bribed into providing early warning as to which block was going to be searched after appell. This was extremely useful, as illicit materials could be moved around and hidden.

The intelligence branch worked very closely with all the factories in supplying intelligence, particularly in the mapmaking and document production units.

Figure 6.1: A typical "Leica" camera of this period.

Communicating Daily News

One of Bushell's directives was to be well informed about what was happening in the theatres of war. A couple of radio operators built a compact and powerful receiver that was cleverly hidden below a toilet. It was used daily while shorthand writers took notes, and these were read to POWs while stooges were posted as lookouts. The radio operators also collected the materials for a radio transmitter, but this was not used in the project.

120

Internal Security

The solution to prowling guards, goons, and ferrets was implemented through a number of well-thought-out measures which all required sophisticated internal security.

Security Zone System

Junior Clark, or Big S, divided the compound into zones, a danger "D" Zone and safe "S" Zone, as shown in Figure 6.2. The D Zone contained the tunnels and factories. As soon as a ferret entered the D Zone, he was tailed. A system of

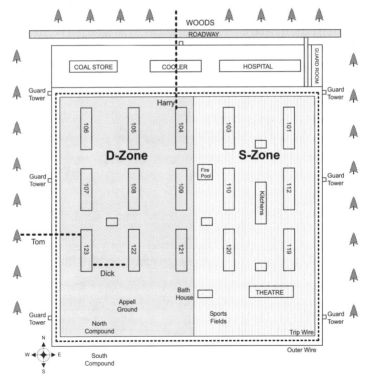

Figure 6.2: The camp was divided into zones, a danger "D" Zone and a safe "S" Zone.

inconspicuous signals warned POWs to hide activities with innocent hobbies. Unable to combat the system, guards allowed it to continue.

Internal Security was always looking for infiltrators or "stool pigeons." They were also responsible for an intercamp semaphore signaling system used for communication between the compounds.

Security Stooge System

The guards and ferrets who prowled the compounds had to be closely monitored. There were a number of English-speaking ferrets, and in the evening they would crawl beneath the huts and listen to conversations inside. Ferrets would also enter empty huts during roll call and hide in the ceilings, so when the POWs returned from appell these ferrets had to be found and cleared out.

The men who monitored guards and ferrets were called "stooges." They watched for those who were getting too close. Every factory had stooges watching for breakthroughs in the general screen and entry into D Zone, and up to 300 POWs operated in shifts. Inconspicuous signals warned POWs to cover up suspicious activities with innocent-looking behavior. The stooges kept their mouths shut and their tedious sentry duty kept the tasks of the rest of the team safe.

An alarm system was set up in the tunnel area. A pebble-filled tin can was gently rattled as a ferret warning. Any descent into the 30-foot (9-meter) vertical shaft leading to the tunnel required a stooge, or lookout, to stand by the door, watching for approaching guards. Tunnelers could shut down the entire operation in less than twenty seconds, and that held true for all the other activities like mapmaking or passport printing or anything else.

Infiltrators or Stool Pigeons

POWs were very sensitive to infiltrators, and all new prisoners coming into the camp had to summon two witnesses to vouch for them. Otherwise, they faced heavy interrogation by senior officers.

Figure 6.3: POWs facing interrogation by fellow POWs.

Intercamp Semaphore Signaling

Between the two compounds, the British (Allied) and the American, a system of intercamp semaphore signaling was set up so they could trade camp news and keep each other updated.

Figure 6.4: Semaphore signaling was set up between the two POW camps.

Dispersal Diversions

The dispersal of sand was probably the biggest problem for the project, and the rate of digging was limited by the rate of dispersal. Diversions were important for diverting the attention of the guards and ferrets away from the sand dispersion. Distractions included events like unarmed combat drills with 40 men fighting or volleyball games with a mob standing around cheering. In another case, a group of 100 men gathered for community singing to drown out the hammering of the toolmakers. Jerry Sage was responsible for dispersal diversions.

Supplies

Willy Williams was the supply chief responsible for "procuring" materials and supplies (foodstuffs) for the project.

Materials for the Tunnel

The volume of materials for the tunnel was significant, specifically the ones used in shoring it up. The supply chief also provided materials for equipment. One source was found within the camp itself: the blocks were scoured for excess materials and bed boards and bedposts were stripped. For example, one of the huts had double boards located under the floorboards. Nails and screws were removed from inside huts, and lead pipes were liberated and used for making molds.

Red Cross Parcels

These packages not only supplemented meager camp food but also were essential to both the escape and post-escape survival outside the camp, which required survival rations. The POWs hoarded Red Cross parcels for the escape.

In addition, Foodacco or "food account" was a currency used for collective bargaining and bartering that allowed POWs to market surplus food for "points" spent on other items.

Figure 6.5: POWs collected and administered Red Cross parcels, hoarding rations for the escape.

Construction of the Tunnel

Tunnel engineering, or tunneling, was the responsibility of Wally Floody, a Canadian fighter pilot and a mining engineer in civilian life. He was also known as the Tunnel King. For a period of time, the project was very dependent on the tunnel with everything revolving around it, and the overall activity required tunnel preparation and engineering.

Trap Doors

Trap door concealment was critical, as the entrance was the most likely part of the tunnel to be discovered. Wally Floody came up with the strategy of passing the tunnels through the brick and concrete foundations around and below the stoves and washrooms. Each of the huts had a room with a small coal stove sitting on a slab of bricks, and the entrance to Harry was tucked beneath a heating stove in Hut 104. The carpenters created a hinged wooden frame and cemented tiles on top of it to replace the former tile foundation. A flexible stovepipe extension was then fashioned. The stove was never without a fire whilst digging was going on, and this discouraged guards from coming too near. From its open position, the trap door could be closed and sealed in twenty seconds using wooden handles on the stove. The tunnel went straight down through the bricks into the ground.

The trap door for Dick from Block 122 was the most ingeniously concealed of the three, hidden beneath an iron grating in the drainage well in the washroom. Water was removed from the drain and a concrete square was cut out of the sidewall and replaced with a specially cast piece sealed in place with a waterproof mixture of clay, soap, and cement. When the trap was closed, water was let in again to the level of the drainage pipe and the grille was replaced.

The traps were so cleverly disguised that when Massey (the SBO) was asked to find and inspect them, he was astonished at how well they were concealed. The traps were operated by "trap fuhrers," each of whom was responsible for monitoring those who entered and exited the respective room and for ensuring the trap could be shut down and disguised before a ferret could walk in and discover it.

Entrance Shafts

Amongst other things, the escape project team had discovered that at depths exceeding 25 feet (8 meters) the listening devices installed by the guards to check tunneling activities were ineffective. As a result, vertical shafts of 30 feet (9 meters) were dropped from the traps, and the tunneling commenced from there. Wooden footholds led down the claustrophobically narrow shaft, past sound-absorbing blankets stuffed around the trap door, and through an initial column of solid brick and concrete that had taken the diggers days to chip away.

Figure 6.6: Entrance shaft to one of the tunnels.

Construction on One Tunnel

Floody assembled thirty-six prisoners to work on the three tunnels in two shifts a day (morning and evening). Twelve tunnelers worked on each tunnel in three-man shifts, so each digger worked two shifts every three days.

The three traps and shafts were finished by the end of May, but Harry and Dick were suspended in June. Bushell decided that all efforts should be concentrated on Tom because of the problem of sand dispersal.

Dispersal Chamber

At the bottom of the shaft, there was an enlargement for a dispersal chamber where the sand brought up from the tunnel face was prepared for dispersal. This receiving area could be used for storing sand, and the bags of sand were prepared for transfer to above ground for dispersion.

Dangers of Digging

The escape committee had identified digging as a high-risk activity. Tunnelers had to dig fast, as the sand was crumbly. The two tunnelers worked in pairs to offset the risk, and they never spoke too much as they were always listening for cracking noises indicating potential subsidence. The tunnelers were trained to pull out as swiftly as possible as the sand could quickly suffocate them.

Many diggers had barely enough time to protect their heads with their arms as the roof suddenly caved in, and they could only hope that their Number Two's could dig them out. No one was killed, but several men were forced to take days off after almost being suffocated. A fall left a large dome above the working face, and after it was cleared up the damaged roof was shored up and the sand packed back above it. The diggers found that sand that had been dug out occupied thirty percent as much space again as it did in its original location, placing extra burdens on the dispersal teams.

Shoring Up the Tunnel

Because sand made up the substrate in which the construction was done, its consistency meant that it was easy to dig but difficult to maintain. The sandy soil required the shafts and tunnels to be shored up with wood, and over 3,000 bed boards and floorboards were removed and used for the shoring. The process involved slotting together the 2-foot-long wooden bed boards to form a box frame structure (61×61 centimeters) using tongue-and-groove assembly, and fitting this into the ceiling, floor, and walls of the tunnel. This dictated the tunnel size as two square feet. To save materials, the frames were spaced one board apart. During a work shift of three tunnelers, one sat at the bottom of the shaft and prepared the stolen bed boards that were slotted together and used to shore up the tunnel's walls and ceiling.

Tunnel Cave-Ins

Even with the shoring, cave-ins at the face of the tunnel were common and occurred every couple of days. A digger risked being buried by 3 feet (1 meter) or 200 pounds (80 kilograms) of sand. Wherever patches of soft sand were found, box frames were placed close together.

Lighting

From the beginning, the underground darkness in the tunnels posed a challenge. At first, the POWs lit the way using homemade mutton-fat lanterns with pajama-fabric wicks, made from grease or fat that was strained from the soup.

One of the electrical engineers rearranged the lighting cable in every hut and ended up with forty pieces of cable from 1 to 10 feet (3 meters) in length. He then spliced the cables together and installed electrical lights in all the shafts.

Ventilation

As the tunnels increased in length, fresh air became more limited underground, so the POWs built an air pump to ventilate the tunnels. The pump consisted of a fabric bellows mounted on wooden runners. The bellows was made from a kit bag ribbed with wooden frames, and its top was sealed around a wooden disk. It was fitted with old boot leather for double inlet and outlet valves (see Figure 6.7).

Figure 6.7: An air pump designed to ventilate the tunnels, consisting of a fabric bellows mounted on wooden runners.

The teams dug out additional large chambers for the air pumps at the foot of the entrance shafts. They then tested the pumps with smoke taken in from burning rags and scoured the system for leaks. This arrangement provided very effective ventilation.

A fourth man was added to the tunnel shift to operate the manual pump back and forth like a rowing machine to pump air through the air lines. For maximum efficiency, the pump forced out air on both the forward and backward strokes. The air lines posed another technical challenge and were made by linking together empty dried-milk tins that were caulked with tape or waxed string. As the tunnel progressed, these ventilation pipes were installed under the tunnel floor at 9 inches/23 cm (see Figure 6.8). A fresh-air intake vent was concealed in Hut 104 with its flue camouflaged into the genuine stove's chimney.

Figure 6.8: The air lines were made from empty dried-milk tins (klim) caulked with tape.

With the air pumps in operation, the tunnel could be closed from the top and the diggers could continue working indefinitely. Every thirty minutes the diggers and pumpers would exchange places so that one set of tired muscles could take a rest for another.

Storage Chamber

The bottom of the shaft was further expanded to provide a storage space to keep extra supplies. During the latter stages of the tunneling, this chamber held items critical to the POWs on escape night, such as forged immigration papers, street clothing, and provisions.

Workshop

This chamber in the shaft served as a manufacturing workshop where specialists made equipment such as digging tools and lamps out of scavenged materials. Here woodworking and metalworking, typically very noisy with tin bashing and filing, could be done in freedom as the noise was well masked.

Railway System

Johnny Travis built a railway to run on small rails to carry men or boxes of sand. The rope-operated trolleys ran up to the face of the tunnel. The rails were made out of wooden beading and battens that had been nailed down. Each trolley had three discs, two larger ones on the outside and a smaller inner disc so it could hug the rail. By nailing tin on the outside of the wheels, the POWs fashioned makeshift tires. Men lay on a trolley, and a rope was used to pull them up to the face without disturbing any of the shoring that lined the tunnel. The railway was an ingenious piece of engineering, as shown in Figure 6.9.

This system revolutionised the sand removal process, allowing diggers to efficiently transport tons of sand from within the tunnel back to its entrance shaft, from where it was later dispersed or buried around the camp.

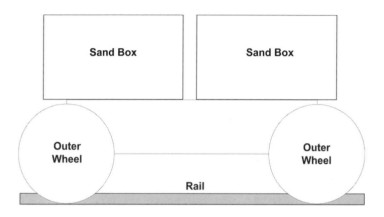

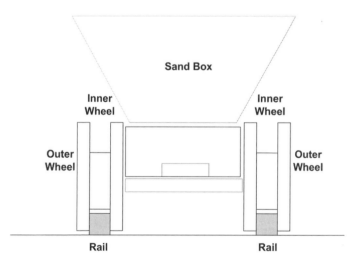

Figure 6.9: The blueprint for the railway, whose design was an ingenious piece of engineering spanning some 300 feet (90 meters).

Sand Removal and Dispersal

The escape committee faced major sand dispersal problems as every 3-4 feet (1 meter) of tunnel generated 1 ton (907 kilograms) of sand. Tunnel sand had to be dispersed very discreetly because it had a different smell from the surface sand and the guard dogs could pick up the scent. It was also a different color. Sand was dug from the tunnel face and stored at the bottom of the shaft, ready for dispersal. The intelligence branch meticulously tracking ferrets would notify the dispersal team when it was all clear for dispersal.

Penguins

Sand dispersal was done through "penguins," POWs who wore long pockets (thin bags) with drawstrings down their pant legs, and these pockets would be filled with sand (approximately 8 pounds or 4 kilograms of sand per sack). After the second appell and during the second shift, the sand collected in the shaft was brought up in metal jugs, so the trap doors had to stay open.

The penguins would go out into the sports area or parts of the camp where gardening was taking place. Other men would create a diversion to distract the guards who were always walking around the wire or watching from the guard towers. The penguins would pull the drawstrings and scuff the sand around and mix it into the ground. At the time, some POWs were cultivating vegetable gardens, and these were very useful for dispersal. Sometimes volleyball games were organised with a large cheering crowd so that sand could be easily shuffled into the ground. Sand was also put in parts of the building, like the attic or hollow walls, but it was more dangerous there because it could be found more easily. A rota of penguins lined up to collect sand and disperse it, at a rate of up to six feet of tunnel per day (1 ton or 907 kilograms). The controllers sent the penguins to different routes to avoid suspicion. At one point, they were disposing of sand at the rate of 60 pounds (30 kilograms) per minute. In all, they made 25,000 sand-dispersing trips.

At this point in the project, a few of the knowledge areas need to be revisited.

Integration Management

This knowledge area (see Table 4.1) covers the integration of all the other eight knowledge areas and includes project plan development, integrated change control, and project execution.

Directing and Managing Project Execution

The departmental chiefs were responsible for their respective departments and guiding and managing their teams towards meeting their departmental project deliverables. Bushell was responsible for the integration of the project components and the overall project deliverables. To support this capacity, he held daily conferences with the escape committee.

Monitoring and Controlling Project Work

The departmental chiefs interacted daily with their teams to discuss progress, issues, and any changes. They were under constant pressure from the fear of being discovered.

Metrics were collected in several areas of the project to help provide a more accurate view of progress. For instance:

- Tunnel length

- Tracking sand dispersal volumes and the number of dispersion trips

- Using the above metrics, they could determine the tunnel length before ventilation was required and assess the volume of air that would have to be pumped in.

- Amount of shoring material being used in the tunnel

Integrated Change Control

Project changes were continuously made according to changing circumstances. Even though changes were tightly controlled, they had to be made at the drop of a hat. For example, it was the responsibility of the escape committee to invoke an immediate response if escape work was detected, and agility was critical. Similarly, German passes and documents changed regularly, so the project's manufactured or acquired papers had to be frequently updated.

Scope Management

This knowledge area (see Table 4.1) plans and defines the scope, identifies major deliverables and the work breakdown structure (WBS), and prepares the organisation's cost-benefit analysis.

Scope Control

In this project, scope was not really an issue as the overall scope was not changed from the three-tunnel plan and the tunnel lengths were known in advance. The escape committee controlled the scope based on the risks. For instance, if one of the tunnels was threatened or under suspicion, work could be halted for that tunnel but continued on another one.

Time Management

This knowledge area (see Table 4.1) defines the activities in the project, completes the activity sequencing, and develops the schedule.

Schedule Control

The escape committee evaluated the activities and their sequencing, duration, and schedule:

- Time to build tunnel, constraints:

    - Manpower available

    - Rate of digging

    - Rate of sand removal, dispersal, and concealment

    - Climate and seasons; spring and summer were tunneling seasons

- Time to prepare escapers:

    - Identities, with adequate documents

    - Disguises, clothes

    - Roles, cover stories, and language acquisition

Cost Management

This knowledge area (see Table 4.1) defines estimates, develops a budget, and controls costs.

Cost Control

The escape committee evaluated the available resources, and these were put under the control of the supplies department, which had some influence over how these could be used (for example, for bribery of guards).

- Food and Parcels
  - Relatives paid for and sent:
    - One parcel per man per week
  - International Red Cross paid for and sent:
    - General distribution–a supply of a single item
    - Replacement clothing, shaving and wash kits, coffee, tea, tinned meat, jam, and sugar distributed equally
  - Captured officers paid:
    - Equivalent of their payout in internal camp currency, used to purchase items like musical instruments

New Compound for American POWs

On June 10 of 1943, construction began on a new compound on the south side of the camp for American POWs who had been crowded into the North Compound with the RAF prisoners and were scheduled to be moved.

Efforts increased on Tom, as no one wanted the Americans in the camp to miss out on the escape. In addition, American POWs were allocated to the factories to learn the intricacies of each one and gain invaluable experience (training) for when they were transferred.

Tunnel Alert

The ferrets had been very suspicious for several weeks after spotting yellow sand before it had been mixed into the surface soil. Work was proceeding at a frantic rate, and the problem of sand dispersal came up again as the department could not risk the ferrets' discovery of more sand. With the expansion of the camp to the west, the escape committee decided that Dick was not really suitable because a new compound was being built over it. Someone came up with the brilliant idea of shoveling surplus sand down this abandoned tunnel. The team would fill in Dick from the face backwards, removing the boards as they went along. This was a good example of how agile the team had to be to take advantage of changing conditions and opportunities. Once the problem of sand dispersal was solved, the rate of digging increased again. Dick was also used for the concealment of equipment.

Communication

The head ferret, suspicious that tunneling was ongoing, asked dozens of POWs the same question related to tunnels so that he could weigh their responses against each other. The escape committee agreed on a consistent response to the ferret's question and communicated this message out to the camp.

Searching Is Increased

For weeks the ferrets increased the frequency and ferocity of searches. Heavy wagons were driven over suspected tunnel areas to force a collapse. The ferrets also probed the ground, sinking long 6-foot (2-meter) rods into the earth, but these were far too short to detect anything. The escape committee braced itself for this level of change and issued special security warnings. The forest to the west of the compound was cut back another 40 feet (12 meters) and tunneling was suspended, as the risks were too great.

Risk Management

This knowledge area (see Table 4.1) makes initial assumptions that affect the project, develops the risk management plan, identifies and analyses risk, plans response and mitigation of the risk, and creates contingency plans.

Risk Monitoring and Control

The escape committee assessed the project risks frequently, especially during the construction phase, and modified the project plans accordingly. The objective was to:

- Assess the probability and impact of risk

- Eliminate risks where appropriate

- Determine new risks since the last meeting

This was a long, complex project fraught with risks, and as the project progressed new risks had to be continually considered, as grouped in Table 6.1 below.

145

Table 6.1: Risk considered by the escape committee as part of continuous risk monitoring and control

Risk: Escaping through the tunnel without incident

Probability	Impact	Mitigation
90%	Many escapers passing through the tunnel could disturb it and cause a collapse	Passing escapers' throughput had to be carefully controlled

Risk: Getting away from the camp unnoticed

Probability	Impact	Mitigation
70%	Being identified as a POW,[11] capture, leading to overall alert.	Disguises, clothing, identification, passes, and plausible roles had to be scrutinized for any flaws (quality control)

Risk: Traveling distances unchallenged

Probability	Impact	Mitigation
40%	Traveling long distances (min. 300 miles)	Using forged passes, having money available, and being able to talk one's way out of a situation

Risk: Surviving in the open

Probability	Impact	Mitigation
60%	Hypothermia or even death	Access to food, water, shelter, and heat

146

Tom Is Found

Tom reached 240 feet (73 meters) and was 40 feet (12 meters) short of the wood but 140 feet (43 meters) outside of the wire. On the 8th of September, after weeks of intensive search, Tom was discovered. This had a profound negative effect on camp morale and on the escape committee, dealing a terrible blow to the POWs psychologically. On the bright side, the ferrets stopped their searching, as they could not believe a second tunnel was in progress after noting the volume of materials required for such a deep and long tunnel. After the discovery, the guards destroyed Tom with explosives.

Aftermath of Tom

German-speaking contacts overheard a conversation between guards who were discussing the tunnel. The exchange indicated that the guards were convinced that there could not be another tunnel underway, considering how such a huge and well-constructed tunnel had been discovered. The contacts also learned that the guards would be checking up on how many bed boards were disappearing from POWs' bunks in the future. This information was immediately conveyed to Bushell, who ordered that bed boards were to be plundered before they could be counted. Many of the 2,000 boards that were collected were hidden down Dick.

Project Focuses on Other Areas

The escape committee wanted to lie low with tunneling activities and suspend all work on the other tunnels, intending to lull the guards into a false sense of security. However, work continued in all the other factories. Losing another tunnel at this point would have been devastating to morale. Besides, winter was the off-season for escaping because rough travel in freezing conditions was considered too dangerous.

Equipment and Toolmaking

All the engineers were added to the equipment and toolmaking factory run by Johnny Travis. He was a walking tool shop, concealing pliers, chisels, and hacksaw blades in his pockets. Because he was a well-dressed officer, the guards considered him an unlikely escaper and didn't bother searching him.

The factory manufactured items for other project teams in the metalworking and carpentry shops. These objects included spades for tunneling, compasses for escape navigation, ventilation pipes for the tunnel, and Luftwaffe insignia made with lead solder from tin cans.

The intelligence men bribed pliable guards for bits of useless metal. These were then worked by filing them away into tools like cold and wood chisels, screwdrivers, and wire cutters. Metal from klim tins was worked into metal strips to make blades and knives that were then fitted into wood frames to make planes. Many materials like nails, screws, and metal tie bars came from the huts in the camp.

Figure 6.10: Replica insignia manufactured with lead solder from tin cans.

The engineers were able to create tools by using a small forge to harden steel and then pouring sugar on top so the carbon was baked into the steel.

Tunneling Tools

Tunneling was done with the crudest homemade tools, typically because the sand was soft and so spades were adequate to dig it.

Concealment

As part of the risk management, the carpenters created numerous hiding spots by building trap doors in walls and floors. In one room the wall was moved out by 9 inches (25 centimeters), but this was impossible to spot unless the room was accurately measured.

Compass Factory

Through bribery, the intelligence branch obtained a magnet for Al Hake and the compass factory. The workers made crude compasses by melting down an old 78-rpm record and forming it into a bowl using a mold and then embedding a gramophone needle in the centre. To this a pivot socket was soldered from the joints in bully-beef tins. A magnetised sewing needle was put into the socket to point north and tipped with luminous paint. Finally, a small circular disk made with glass from the windows was set into the casing (see Figure 6.11).

Figure 6.11: A compass made by Al Hake's factory, waterproof and luminous in the dark.

Mapmaking

The intelligence branch was able to supply the mapmaking organisation with much-needed information about the outlying regions around the camp. With this they were able to create an accurate map including all the paths, the size of the surrounding woods, and a layout of the local town. A staff of map tracers forged general maps that showed escape routes to Czechoslovakia and Switzerland and from the Baltic to Sweden. With hundreds of maps to make, tracing was too slow by hand. Des Plunkett created a "mimeograph," a simple copying machine operated by hand-pressing paper to a gelatin press, with the map outlined with crushed pencil leads. This machine produced around 4,000 local and strip maps of routes. The mapmakers also created large-scale escape maps out of rice paper and sewed them into clothing.

Figure 6.12: A pack of cards concealing an escape map.

151

Document Production

All the artists were added to the forgery factory run by Tim
Walenn. A complex part of the project required production
materials like paper and ink. One of the contacts persuaded a
guard to bring in nibs, ink, and paper under the pretext of
wanting to take up drawing to pass the time.

Quality Control

The biggest challenge facing the department was that official
stamps and the appearance of the various papers were changed
regularly, and many of the modifications required weeks to
reproduce (see Figure 6.13). Over fifty forgers (mainly artists)
and stooges worked three to five hours per day for a year.
They had to sit by the windows, working meticulously until
they had headaches, as one careless slip could cost four days of
work on one document. Any forgery that was not perfect was
scrapped, and this is where project quality control came in.

Supplies

Getting hold of paper was a problem for the POWs. Better-
quality paper was taken from bibles, and the prisoners made
more paper by gluing tracing linen onto cardboard and then
tinting it with watercolours. To further authenticate
correspondence, a letterhead professing to be from the nearby
Focke Wulf Factory was produced. Typewritten sheets were
recreated by hand, and this was done so well that the forgeries
were indistinguishable from the original documents.

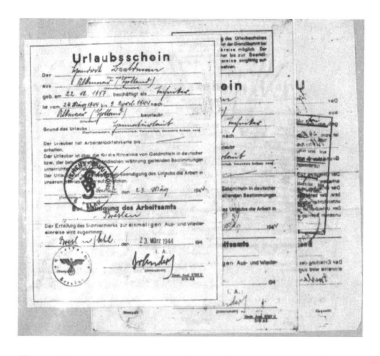

Figure 6.13: A selection of output from the forgery factory including passes and documents that were indistinguishable from the originals.

Automation

Various techniques were used to speed up production. For example, Johnny Travis made a tiny printing press, using a carved piece of wood covered in a strip of blanket for a roller. One calligrapher recreated stencils of the official Nazi stamps (the eagle and swastika) on rubber boot heels, and documents carrying identification photos were endorsed with these impressions. Al Hake's compass group cut these stamps out of the boot heels to create really authentic-looking passes. This work had to be done very meticulously as it would be put to close scrutiny.

In all, over four hundred forged papers were required, and this included passports with photos, passes for excursions like military leave, *Solbuch* cards (general identity cards combined with pay books), papers granting permission to be on Wehrmacht property, and documents for foreign workers returning home. Necessary paperwork also included paper currency, visas, and letters of introduction or authorisation, such as those for employees traveling on business to locations like Stettin or Danzig (both docked neutral Swedish ships).

With characteristic good-natured humour, the mapmaking and document production teams were known jointly as "Dean and Dawson," a well-known firm of travel agents.

Passport Photos

There was a need to create identification photos for passports, and for this a camera and film had to be procured. The theatre played a vital role in this process, especially as there were a number of London West End producers, actors, and technical people in the camp. The productions were excellent and German officers always wanted to see the plays, so the front two rows were reserved for them. The POWs took advantage of this enthusiasm for the theatre and asked if the plays could be recorded for history. They were provided with film and a camera to take pictures of the productions, but of course most of the film was used for making passport photos and documents. With a camera now available, the project team created a photo unit complete with a photo studio.

Production of Clothing

Once the POWs had escaped from the camp, they would need disguises to travel incognito on the outside, and this required the production of clothing. Through bribery, the intelligence branch obtained thread, buttons, and bits of cloth for Tommy Guest and the clothing factory. Anyone who could sew was added to the clothing department team.

The POWs' uniforms were altered to create new clothing. For instance, uniforms of heavy serge (a type of twill fabric) were shaved with razor blades and died using beetroot juice or boot polish solutions. The uniforms were then carefully recut by the department into workmen's' clothes and other civilian attire. There were thousands of foreign workers traveling around the area, so this was a good disguise. Even German uniforms, complete with fake weapons, were made from blankets and Allied uniforms.

As there were so many uniforms to convert, paper patterns were cut from German newspapers and passed to POWs to make their own alterations. Within the camp, civilian garments were strictly forbidden and genuine civilian items of clothing were carefully hidden. Escapees always secretly carried aircrew badges whilst escaping to prove they were not spies. The Geneva Convention dictated that servicemen always wear uniforms.

155

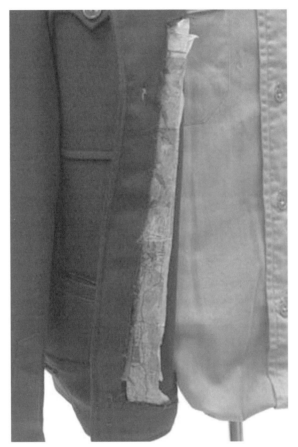

Figure 6.14: Converted uniforms had secret maps sown into the lining

Quality Management

This knowledge area (see Table 4.1) plans the approach to quality in a project, identifies the required quality characteristics, and builds the quality assignments into the schedule.

Performing Quality Assurance

Projects need to provide evidence that they are conforming to a quality assurance process. This evidence typically consists of project work products and is made available to the quality inspector to confirm compliance.

Previous escape attempts gave the escape committee invaluable experience and helped highlight the details of a plot that could fail. Quality assurance was done at a local level within the functions, but inspections also took place through the escape committee and Little S. This built-in quality testing had to be done from the project outset.

Performing Quality Control

Typically done through work product inspections, quality control is an important mechanism for effective early defect identification and removal. It is also known as static testing or peer reviews, and it includes inspections and document reviews of critical work products. The emphasis is on inspections of all critical work products "early and often," with all team members participating in these assessments.

The escape committee realised that mistakes were intolerable and that quality had to be brought into every activity, as even one slip-up would give the game away. For example:

- Tunnel construction had to be done in secrecy and with safety.

- Forged documents would be scrutinised, so they had to be perfect.

- Clothing had to meld the wearer inconspicuously into a crowd.

- The evening shift in the tunnel used compasses and spirit levels to gauge whether the tunnel was set true to north and perfectly straight and level.

Keeping the Project Going

The scale of the whole operation, the number of factories, and the scope of their activities presented a security problem in keeping everything hidden. As a result, the factories were constantly being moved around blocks when the situation got too hot.

Project Tracking

Although at any point up to six hundred POWs were working on the project, only twelve men knew the minute details of it. Bushell met his departmental chiefs daily to share status reports so that resources could be closely managed and risks could be better mitigated.

Harry Is Reopened

In January of 1944, Bushell wanted work to resume on Harry. He thought that it would be best to concentrate on that one tunnel, but the principal problem still lay in the dispersal of sand. He sent his chiefs away with instructions to come up with a solution.

Mitigating Risk

Sand dispersal was still the biggest risk. Eventually it dawned on one of the POWs that there was a huge closed-off area under the 350 seats of the theatre. Some time before, the guards had allowed the theatre to be built, using tools and equipment supplied on parole. Parole was a written promise of a POW to fulfill stated conditions in exchange for certain privileges, and it usually carried a threat of death if violated. Although the equipment for the theatre construction was never

Figure 6.15: The theatre built by POWs using wood from red cross boxes was very much supported by the Kommandant.

used for other purposes and the POWs could probably gain access to it unnoticed, the parole system was regarded as inviolate and there was hesitancy about defying it.

Internal "legal advice" was taken, and the SBO's decision was that the popular and very successful theatre itself did not fall within the parole system. Seat 13 was therefore hinged and camouflaged, and the vast space beneath it was used for sand dispersal.

Tunneling Resumes on Harry

In January of 1944, the team recommenced work on Harry, tunneling beyond the 140 feet (42 meters) that had already been dug. Lessons learned from the discovery of Tom were applied to the work on Harry. For instance, the underground railway trolley system was installed, and it eventually shifted about 130 tons (118,000 kilograms) of the estimated 200 tons (181,000 kilograms) of sand.

To the authorities, Harry's location seemed the least likely one for a tunnel, as it lay under both the wire and the *Vorlager*, a garrison area that contained the sick quarters, the Red Cross parcel store, and the cooler (see Figure 5.3). The tunnel then had to go under another set of wires and across open ground into the wood. In all, it calculated out to be about 350 feet (110 meters).

Sand Disposal

The method for discarding sand was improved considerably. The sand was still collected after the second appell, but it was brought up in a kit bag rather than in metal jugs. The kit bags were then carried directly to the theatre during a four-hour period in the evening when traffic was heavy and this activity was not likely to raise suspicions.

Lighting

The lanterns that were being used in the tunnel proved to be noxious and unreliable, so the team found a way to use electricity to illuminate Harry. During the summer, two intrepid POWs liberated (snatched) 800 feet (240 meters) of electrical wire from workmen who were wiring speakers for the camp radio. The whole tunnel was strung with lights and the power was tapped from the camp supply through Stalag Luft III's circuit board. This system provided lighting for the night shift when the power was turned on.

Crossing Points

These were built every 100 feet (30 meters) along the railway. Piccadilly Circus was the first of Harry's two halfway changeover stations, each a third of the way along the tunnel. There, POWs would transfer themselves to a new trolley for the next leg, whether heading back or going forward. With variations in the tunnel, it was possible that ropes over 100 feet (30 meters) in length could rub against the shoring, and hence the stations were vitally important. The POWs called the second changeover station Leicester Square.

161

Searches Continue

Over time, the ferrets became suspicious and once again presumed that a tunnel was in progress. At one point they brought in a diviner who, in the absence of any telltale tremors, failed to find the tunnel even whilst walking directly over it.

Snap appells were introduced as authorities tried to catch the POWs underground in the process of tunneling. As a precaution, new procedures were introduced to ensure that the tunnel could be evacuated at a moment's notice.

Kugel Order

The camp Kommandant called in the senior officers, doctors, and chaplains to explain the changing situation in the Third Reich and the public intolerance to Allied airmen. The *Kugel* (bullet) Order decreed that captured POWs would be taken to a concentration camp to be gassed or shot.

Project Team Disrupted

The guards were aware that something major was going on, but all attempts to discover the tunnel failed. In a desperate move, nineteen top suspects, including six key men in the project, were transferred with no warning to the nearby Stalag VIIIC at Belaria, only weeks before the escape was scheduled to take place. The relocated men included Wally Floody, the Tunnel Chief. Bushell's part in the escape committee was well camouflaged, and the guards left him behind. He had gone to great efforts to show that he was of reformed character; for example, he became heavily involved in the theatre and was by

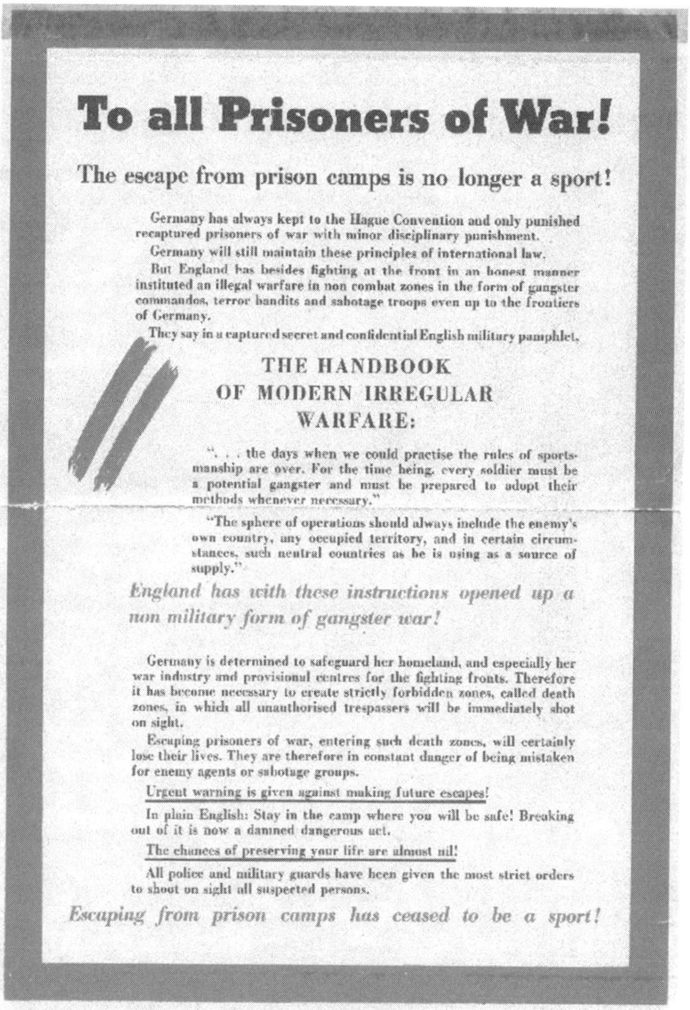

To all Prisoners of War!

The escape from prison camps is no longer a sport!

Germany has always kept to the Hague Convention and only punished recaptured prisoners of war with minor disciplinary punishment.

Germany will still maintain these principles of international law.

But England has besides fighting at the front in an honest manner instituted an illegal warfare in non combat zones in the form of gangster commandos, terror bandits and sabotage troops even up to the frontiers of Germany.

They say in a captured secret and confidential English military pamphlet,

THE HANDBOOK
OF MODERN IRREGULAR
WARFARE:

". . . the days when we could practise the rules of sportsmanship are over. For the time being, every soldier must be a potential gangster and must be prepared to adopt their methods whenever necessary."

"The sphere of operations should always include the enemy's own country, any occupied territory, and in certain circumstances, such neutral countries as he is using as a source of supply."

England has with these instructions opened up a non military form of gangster war!

Germany is determined to safeguard her homeland, and especially her war industry and provisional centres for the fighting fronts. Therefore it has become necessary to create strictly forbidden zones, called death zones, in which all unauthorised trespassers will be immediately shot on sight.

Escaping prisoners of war, entering such death zones, will certainly lose their lives. They are therefore in constant danger of being mistaken for enemy agents or sabotage groups.

Urgent warning is given against making future escapes!

In plain English: Stay in the camp where you will be safe! Breaking out of it is now a damned dangerous act.

The chances of preserving your life are almost nil!

All police and military guards have been given the most strict orders to shoot on sight all suspected persons.

Escaping from prison camps has ceased to be a sport!

Figure 6.16: Kugel (bullet) Order decreed that captured POWs would be taken to a concentration camp to be gassed or shot.

all accounts a very good actor. Deputies took over for the missing POWs, and the work on the escape continued.

Tunnel Is Completed

The chief ferret was away for two weeks in early March, so the risk of discovery was slightly reduced. This gave the escape committee an incentive to increase their efforts, and during the first nine days of March diggers cleared the last 100 feet (30 meters) of the tunnel. Progress had been rapid and Harry, with a final length of 348 feet (116 meters) from shaft to face, was completed in around two months. As the surveyors had estimated that it was 335 feet (112 meters) to the edge of the wood, the team believed that Harry ran underneath the wooded area. Some 130 tons (118,000 kilograms) of sand were disposed of under seats of the theatre.

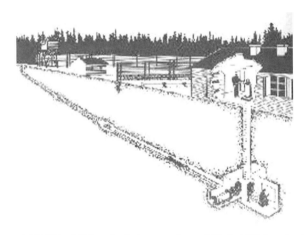

Figure 6.17: The full length of the tunnel was 348 feet (116 meters) reaching the woods.

Exit Shaft

By March 14, the diggers created an exit shaft by digging upward almost to the surface, placing boards across the span, and shoring up the tunnel. Digging 30 feet (9 meters) straight up was extremely dangerous and yet it had to be done. On the night of the escape, 2 feet (0.6 meters) of earth was to be removed, but when they tested the depth to the surface there was only 6 inches (15 centimeters) of dirt above because the ground sloped off.

Materials Required

A huge number of materials were used for Harry:

- 4,000 bed boards
- 34 chairs
- 52 20-man tables
- 90 double-tier bunks
- 1,370 beading battens
- 1,212 bed bolsters
- 10 single tables
- 76 benches
- 1,699 blankets
- 635 palliasses
- 1,219 knives
- 478 spoons

- 582 forks

- 69 lamps

- 30 shovels

- 1,000 feet (304 meters) of electric wire

- 600 feet (183 meters) of rope

- 161 pillowcases

- 192 bedcovers

- 3,424 towels

- 246 water cans.

This was a considerable amount of material for a camp of six hundred POWs, and the fact that this volume of goods was utilised attests to both the resourcefulness of the supplies department and the willingness of the POWs to endure hardship for an important common cause.

Survival Rations

With escape night in sight, a number of cooks prepared baked iron rations by mixing a "fudge" concoction that was poured into small, pocket-sized tins and intended as survival food. This fudge was a compound of sugar, cocoa, condensed milk, raisins, oats, glucose, margarine, chocolate, and ground biscuits. One 4-ounce (100-gram) tin held enough calories to sustain a POW for two days.

Simultaneously, engineers from the equipment and toolmaking factories switched their efforts to the manufacture of water bottles by cutting food tins into sheets and making them into flat flasks.

Figure 6.18: Cooks prepare baked iron rations by mixing a "fudge" concoction for the escape.

Scope Management

This knowledge area (see Table 4.1) plans and defines the scope, identifies major deliverables and the work breakdown structure (WBS), and conducts the organisation's cost-benefit analysis.

Scope Verification

Client inspections and approval of major deliverables are considered part of quality control and acceptance criteria. In the escape project, the clients or beneficiaries were the POWs and the members of the escape committee.

Conclusions

In project construction, the first step is to complete the detailed design, followed by construction and testing of the solution. During this phase, the project suffered an almost fatal setback with the discovery of Tom. Many activities stopped, and it looked as if the project would be shut down permanently. The tunnels required a huge number of physical resources and a great deal of personal sacrifice on the part of the POWs who gave up their possessions for the sake of the project. The discovery was a great blow to the POWs and their morale, and it is a testament to their determination and resilience that they did not give up on the project. Typically, in such a situation a project would be shut down, but because the POWs planned for such a scenario they had an alternative strategy that they could readily adopt. They had identified and quantified the risk of having a tunnel found, and so they had begun digging three of them to provide a fallback plan in case of discovery. When the risk event materialised, they used their risk response plan to hold off on further tunneling until things cooled down and the work could resume. Yet all the while they continued working on non-tunneling activities in order to preserve the project schedule as much as possible. The multiple-tunnel approach was an example of brilliant planning up front.

As the project continued to progress through this phase, the escape committee was dealing with a phenomenal amount of change and was continuously managing and accommodating the risk. The escape committee was eventually able to remove each obstacle it came across. Ideas and solutions were continually tested and refined in a determined atmosphere where everything was thought possible. The approach was one of continuous improvisation and improvement, and Bushell's management style promoted this mindset by effectively selecting leaders and letting them get on with their work. For example, the railway was an innovation that dramatically improved the efficiency of the whole operation many times over. This is an important philosophy for today's projects, where problems are proactively solved through a determined approach that requires an experienced and innovative team to be responsive and willing to try new options.

CHAPTER SEVEN

Implementation and Breakout

"The weather's going to be bloody awful, and will probably get worse. Ninety percent of the hardarsers will run into deep snow in the mountains...[but it]...Doesn't matter. It will give the Nazis an almighty shock. Two hundred looney escape artists roaring around the countryside." Conversation between Roger Bushell and Wings Day prior to the escape on March 23, 1944[5]

This chapter looks at the implementation of the project: the escape through the tunnel and the breakout from the camp.

171

Scope Management

Typically, a project will revisit this knowledge area (see Table 4.1) and review major deliverables, the work breakdown structure (WBS), and the organisation's cost-benefit analysis.

Scope Planning

This phase actively plans the work for future deliverables, but the scope needs to be achievable with resources at hand. Otherwise, the project could get into trouble. When the escape committee started to plan the escape, they were instigating a project of a monumental scale, a one-time escape. In this situation, the tunnel was going to be used only once, so there were no future deliverables.

Breakout

On March the 15th of 1944, eleven months after the escape plan had been put into place, Harry was ready. The ferrets, convinced that a tunnel existed, continued with intensive searches of the huts, and the escape committee members were very worried about its discovery.

Profiling POWs

The project had to determine who was going to escape, in what order they would escape, and how specific resources would be allocated to the escapees.

Selecting Escapers

How were people selected to go? Almost six hundred men had helped with the work, and it was an invidious task to decide who should share in the reward. The escape committee nominated seventy of the escapers from among those who had contributed most to the project, and Bushell selected another twenty he believed to be most deserving.

Balloting

Anyone who had worked on the tunnel in any capacity could be selected by lot. There were five hundred applications from would-be escapers, and ballots were held to whittle down this number.

Two Groups of Escapers

Altogether two hundred and twenty would-be escapers were divided into two groups:

- Around six escapers had vital information and first-rate escape plans that offered a very good chance of their getting back to England, and these men were given the first six spots. The remaining twenty or so places went to those whose personal characteristics gave them the best shot at success. These were German speakers and experienced escapers who had been out before and stood a good chance of making a "home run" to England with the help of good plans. They were given top priority for resources and were issued forged train tickets, forged papers and travel documents, and civilian clothes, typically suits (up to fifty suits were made for the train travelers). These men also enjoyed the benefit of higher places in the exit order, and as a result they had more time before the alarm went off. They were expected to travel by train, masquerading as foreign workers. Germany at the time was flooded with genuine foreign workers, who often spoke no German and carried papers that were frequently out of order.

- The "hardarsers" who filled the rest of the tunnel places were planning to lie up and hide by day and footslog by night over hundreds of miles of enemy territory. They would create a diversion to enable the top escapers to get away. Equipped with only the most rudimentary false papers and identities, this group of men knew that their chances in winter were thin. Snow still lay on the ground and the nighttime temperature was below freezing.

The Escape

The chief ferret returned and ordered a four-hour search of Hut 104, the home of Harry. The escape committee was very nervous after the loss of Tom, and Bushell was determined to break out at the next opportunity. Unfortunately, the weather was not in the least ideal, as the ground was covered with six inches (15 cm) of snow, and it showed every likelihood of getting worse. There were four conditions Bushell wanted for the night of the planned escape:

- No moon

- A wind to mask noises

- Good weather

- No ferrets around

The next possible moonless nights were March 23, 24, and 25, although the 25th was a Saturday, which meant reduced train service. The escape committee debated whether to go, and there were strong arguments for postponing the escape until April brought the expected better weather. However, the tunnelers shared Bushell's concern that Harry would not survive the wet month of April. Any heavy downpour could put pressure on the structure of the tunnel and cause it to collapse.

The escapers had to wait one week. One idea that was put forward and accepted by the escape committee was to put one seasoned escaper between every twenty escapers so that if things did go wrong they could get the escape moving again.

Poor Conditions

Winter was really not a good time to make an escape, especially for the many hardarsers who would have to travel cross-country without the comforts of a train journey.

Decision to Proceed

On March 23rd there was an escape committee meeting to discuss the escape. There was a lot of concern for the hardarsers whose chances were put at 100 to 1 against them. Someone proposed that they put out a few of the train travelers and then close the tunnel up, but this idea was rejected.

On March 24th at 11:30 a.m., Bushell was walking around the camp with Wing Commander "Wings" Day, determining whether to go ahead with the escape plot. Postponement for the night actually meant a month's delay, because the darkness of a new moon and its advantages for concealment would be lost. POW morale would likely slump, and the probability for discovery of the escape plot would increase.

The decision was very difficult for Bushell because he knew the stakes had been raised, but he made up his mind and insisted that they proceed, despite the known risk. The order was given and the forgery team stamped Friday's date onto all of the papers.

The tunnel was 30 feet (9 meters) deep and extended 348 feet (104 meters) beyond the wire. There were two hundred and twenty men scheduled to crawl to freedom on that cold, snowy March night.

176

Integration Management

This knowledge area (see Table 4.1) covers the integration of all the other eight knowledge areas and includes project plan development, integrated change control, and project execution.

Final Preparations

The escapers prepared to go on the night of March 24/25th, 1944. The escape would start at 9 p.m. and continue to 5:30 a.m., allowing over 8.5 hours or 510 minutes to get two hundred and twenty escapers out. This meant one escaper was to break out every two to three minutes.

Tunnels

To ensure the escape was done in silence, strips of blanket were torn and placed over the rails to muffle the noise of POWs shuffling along the train tracks.

Equipment

The Little Xs handed out the equipment that had been carefully stored in hiding places, including water bottles, maps, compasses, and papers.

Marshalls

Marshalls were each assigned ten men and given the task of preparing them and ensuring they had everything they needed. Everything had to add up, from the fake names to the backgrounds to the disguises, and mannequin parades were held so that each escaper could be scrutinised for the smallest details. Marshalls carried out in-depth mock interrogations that tested the escapers' cover stories with complex questions.

POWs who were not breaking out were moved to other huts, and those who were escaping were crowded into Hut 104 as carefully as possible, so that the guards would not notice. The POWs were on edge but quite optimistic. Nervously, those selected to go gathered in the hut in their civilian clothes. One of them caused great consternation when he arrived in the hut dressed as a German soldier. The disguise was that perfect.

Breakout

At 9.30 p.m. on 24 March 1944, Bushell gave the order to go and Harry was opened up. The railway swiftly ferried the POWs through Harry to the exit shaft.

Various Things Go Wrong

In the implementation phase, things started to go seriously wrong almost immediately, and the POWs had to improvise their way around these problems.

Frozen Trap Door

The first escaper found the exit trap door frozen solid, which delayed things as he struggled to open it. At 10:15 p.m. the escapers began to move through the tunnel, and the first escaper emerged out of the exit at 10.30 p.m., well behind schedule.

Tunnel Too Short

When the first escapers broke through the exit, they discovered that the tunnel was not as long as they had anticipated and was nearly 20 feet (6 meters) short of its intended mark. Its exit shaft cleared the prison's perimeter fence but did not make it to the cover of trees beyond. It was within 45 feet (14 meters) of a guard tower on the edge of the prison camp, and this meant there was a high risk of discovery, especially when the escapers' dark figures were profiled against the snow.

Improvisation

Word quickly got back to Bushell about the problem. Clever improvisation was required to continue with the escape, as sentries circled outside the wire and passed the escape exit at intervals. A signaling system was set up to signal to POWs when they could safely come up. This was done using a rope, with one end held outside by a spotter POW hidden behind a ferret bush and the other end passed down the exit hole. The POW in the exit shaft would tug the rope, and if the coast was clear the spotter would give one tug, and if not he would give two tugs. This is a good example of agile thinking, but it was a split-second operation and the passage of escapers was greatly slowed down. On top of that, the escapees left a visible trail in the snow.

Air Raid

The situation worsened when an RAF bombing raid began on Berlin. As a result, the power to the camp, and therefore to the tunnel as well, was cut off between 12 and 1 a.m. No escapers could go out, and the POWs resorted to using fat lanterns instead.

Cave-Ins

At 1:30 a.m. an escaper fell off the trolley, and as he was repositioning himself a 3-foot (1-meter) section of the roof collapsed. It took over one hour to repair the tunnel.

At 2:30 a.m. a decision was made to put through only one hundred escapers, and the final hundred men were told to abandon the escape.

At 2:45 a.m. the last of the "suitcase brigade" got through, and the "blanket brigade" took its turn. With each of them carrying a single rolled blanket tied around his neck, many escapers ran into problems as the blankets were too long and became jammed between themselves and the tunnel walls.

Many had so much food and kit items packed on them that they had to be slimmed down. The bulky packs of some of the men got caught in the wooden lining of the tunnel as they were hauled along the way, and dislodged sand fell onto the tracks. The blanket brigade went out in groups, each group being led by a fluent German speaker.

Throughput

The rate was expected to be sixty men per hour, with hopes of getting two hundred and twenty prisoners out. By 2 a.m. the actual rate was twelve men per hour and only thirty escapers had made it out, well under the expected two hundred. In the first four hours, only fifty prisoners got through and there were only three hours of darkness left, so word was sent back to the hut that it was likely that only a hundred or so could escape.

Guard Stumbles onto Escape

Over the next few hours, the rate did not improve. Things went much slower than expected and there were only eighty-seven escapers out by 4:55 a.m. After many close calls, an escaper at the mouth of the tunnel confused the one-tug, all-clear signal with the two-tug, stay-put signal and emerged from the exit at an inopportune moment. At the same time, a guard who was supposed to be patrolling the wire decided to answer a call of nature. Standing at the edge of the woods, he was startled when a head popped out between his legs. He fired his rifle and more POWs emerged from behind the trees, hands up. The escape had been discovered and the rest of the operation was aborted.

Alarm Is Sounded

As the guard blew his whistle, the camp sprang to life with shouts and the barking of search dogs. Down in the tunnel, the waiting men scrambled quickly back to Hut 104, terrified that a guard would enter through the tunnel exit and fire shots. They burned their false papers and ate the carefully saved rations. Many of them were bitterly disappointed and livid with anger.

Appell

The whole camp was taken out into the square where the guards counted frantically, trying to establish who had escaped. Some prisoners were sent back through the tunnel from the exit and emerged in Hut 104. The men who were part of the escape tried to mingle with the rest of the POWs on the parade ground, but they were recognised too and put into the cooler shortly afterwards.

The guards were very angry upon discovering the escape, more so when they found that eighty men had climbed out of the long tunnel and seventy-six of them had already got away. A search for the escaped POWs began on the outside.

National Alert

The impact of the escape was spectacular, and the highest possible alert in the Third Reich was sounded. *Grossfahndung* (national alert) was ordered and Gestapo police, troops, and *Landwacht* (Home Guard) were mobilised to respond. An estimated 70,000 men were involved in the search, and the whole countryside was rallied to catch the escapers.

Conclusions

There are a number of key points to consider in the implementation phase. First, the decision to proceed was extremely controversial and recognised as the most difficult one for Bushell. There was no one else who could make the decision, as it was his project, but he also had a tremendous vested interest as he had a burning desire to escape. Clearly, there was a conflict of interest, and he knew he was putting a lot of POWs' lives at risk. Bushell had supreme authority to the point of rewarding people with a priority place in the escape queue. In today's world, it is essential that project managers are not put in positions of ultimate authority when there are conflicting priorities and personal conflicts of interest.

Second, the core of the project team, the escape committee including Bushell, was out of the tunnel very early, so problems encountered later were left to other POWs to solve.

Third, even though the escape had been planned in meticulous detail and this strategy looked good, the escape ran into problems right from the outset of the implementation, including a very serious issue with the tunnel being too short. There was a clear lack of contingency planning in not building the tunnel longer, just to be sure. Despite these problems, the escapers continued with a high level of optimism and a spirit of improvisation, but the throughput rate of escape was dramatically slower than expected. In reality, the implementation had not really been well thought through or tested.

So in hindsight, what could have been done differently? There could have been testing through a dry run of the implementation, by actually taking groups of POWs through the tunnel. Had the exit shaft been opened in advance, the escape committee would have been aware of the shortfall in length, and contingency plans could have been drawn for this. Testing may also have flushed out some of the potential but unenvisioned problems like the blackout void, the tunnel collapse, and so on.

CHAPTER EIGHT

Closing: A Project Success or Failure?

"Part of our mission was to divert the Germans, and we did that. They had almost 70,000 men out looking for the escapees within a day of the escape, so we felt that in itself was a sufficient diversion for the Germans." George McKiel, POW[5]

This chapter reviews the project aftermath, considers whether the project was a success or failure, and completes a postmortem. It revisits the factors in Chapter 1: fear of failure that prevents projects from getting off the ground, measures to reduce risk, and ways to make projects more palatable.

Aftermath

Huge numbers of troops and civilians were engaged in the search and roundup of escapees, so in this respect alone the escape had succeeded in hindering the German war effort.

Who Made It

Within days, most of the escapees were recaptured. Around seventy-six of the two hundred and twenty made it out of the camp, but seventy-three were recaptured. During the blackout, escapers could not find the railway station, and as a result they missed their trains. Much praise is due to the hardarsers who knew that their chances in winter were thin. Everyone was rounded up in two weeks except three escapers who made it to a neutral country and achieved the elusive "home run." These were two Norwegians who reached neutral Sweden and a Dutchman who reached Gibraltar via France and Spain (in six weeks).

The recaptured escapers were taken to the Gestapo on Himmler's orders. This was unusual, as recaptured POWs were normally handed over to the civilian police to be dealt with accordingly. The POWs were then interrogated and moved between prisons.

Roger Bushell never made it to the freedom of neutral land, even though he had a very good escape plan and was heading to Czechoslovakia to get out through the Balkans. He almost made it, but at the border a minor discrepancy on one of his papers gave him away.

Reprisal

The Luftwaffe had been responsible for the administration and guarding of the camp. After the escape, they were immediately replaced by the SS, who came in with submachine guns. About three weeks later, Group Captain H. Massey, the SBO, was summoned by the new commander. The Kommandant told him that there was some sad news in that some of the officers had tried to escape and were shot in the process. When he asked the Kommandant how many were wounded and was told, "None," the SBO knew that the prisoners had been executed.

Singly or in small groups, the POWs were taken from civilian or military prisons, driven to remote locations, and shot whilst taking advantage of an offered chance to relieve themselves. The Gestapo groups submitted almost identical reports stating, "The POWs, whilst relieving themselves, broke for freedom and were shot whilst trying to escape." This infamous expression has now passed into history as a euphemism for cold-blooded murder.

The POWs found out later that the Gestapo had carried out the executions. The men had been taken in small groups and shot in the back of the head and then cremated. Their ashes were returned to the POWs. It was a real shock to the camp inmates, and even the Kommandant was aghast at what had happened. He and his officers were very opposed to what the SS had done, and they did their utmost to disassociate themselves from the murders. They allowed the POWs to build a local memorial to the murdered men, a stone cairn to inter the ashes.

Figure 8.1: The 50 POWs executed by the Gestapo.

Figure 8.2: The POWs built a local memorial to the murdered men.

188

Success or Failure?

Was the project a success? Looking at the facts on the plus side, it caused massive disruption to the German forces, one of Bushell's objectives, and around 70,000 men were out looking for the escapees within a day of the escape, if only for a few days. On the down side, too few POWs made it out of Stalag Luft III and too few had got away from Sagan. Tragically, fifty were executed and eight were sent to concentration camps.

The escape deeply stunned the community of POWs all over Germany, whilst back in Stalag Luft III one man tried to kill himself, consumed with guilt over the escape. So was it all worth it? For most of the POWs there was little question, as evident in this quote:

> "Part of our mission was to divert the Germans, and we did that. They had almost 70,000 men out looking for the escapees within a day of the escape, so we felt that in itself was a sufficient diversion for the Germans. In that respect, we felt they paid a dear price—that we had done our jobs. But we paid a dear price, too. We had fifty good men executed, and that was a very painful thing indeed."
> George McKiel, POW[5]

Closing the Project

This particular project closed with the escape. However, in some escapes the route could be reused, so the project would not shut down but continue with other iterations and deliveries.

Postmortem

To further determine why the project was not a complete success and pinpoint exactly what went wrong, the following section outlines the three steps in a postmortem (see Figure 8.3):

1. *Discovery*—What went wrong? What should have/ have not happened but did not/did happen? For this step, you need to perform the following procedures:

   - Create the problem statement
   - Collect the evidence (metrics)
   - Determine contributing factors

2. *Analysis*—Why did it go wrong? What were the contributing factors? What were the root causes of the contributing factors? For this step, you need to perform the following procedures:

   - Categorise the events
   - Analyse the root causes of the events

3. *Corrective Actions*—How can the project team prevent the outcome from going wrong again? What lessons are there for projects today? For this step, you need to perform the following procedures:

- Identify corrective actions to root causes

- Evaluate your organisation's ability to run the project

- Implement the changes

Figure 8.3: The three steps of a project postmortem, which all projects should undergo regardless of the outcome.

Discovery Step

What went wrong? What should have/have not happened but did not/did happen? For this step, you need to perform the following procedures:

- Create the problem statement

- Collect the evidence (metrics)

- Determine contributing factors

In the Discovery Step the problem statement and the determination of the contributing factors must take into account any supporting evidence (available through metrics).

Creating a timeline of events (see Table A.1) requires the identification of the events that had the most impact on the outcome, those thought to be "problematic," before starting to focus on the timeline and root causes. Determining these events requires the careful definition of a problem statement, as there might be ambiguity as to what the problem is or whether several problems occurred simultaneously.

For example, a first question about the Great Escape's outcome might be, "Why did only three POWs reach safety?" The simple answer is that they ran out of luck. However, it is important to phrase the question in a meaningful context (in this case, the tragic loss of life), so that the question reads, "Why did the Great Escape have a tragic outcome, with so many lives lost?" The emphasis is on learning lessons.

A good problem statement helps to determine the contributing factors to the Great Escape's outcome:

1. Enemy tolerance for escapers was very low.

2. The escape committee pressed on with the plan despite mounting problems.

3. The majority of POWs (with the exception of fifteen) were poorly equipped for difficult conditions.

The later Analysis Step of the postmortem provides a

detailed analysis that will lead to the root causes of the outcome to determine why it went wrong. Before you can proceed to that step, however, you must first identify the events that had the most impact on the outcome, or were most "problematic" (see Table A.1) as related to the contributing factors. For example, for contributing factor 1 (enemy tolerance for escapers was very low), these events were:

a) An increase in public attacks and disturbances directed at Allied airmen parachuting onto targets on German soil (see D1.1 in Table A.1)

b) The Kugel order was published

c) POWs received a warning from the Kommandant, only one of many issued (see E3.1 in Table A.1)

For contributing factor 2 (the escape committee pressed on with the plan despite mounting problems), the leaders continued with the escape although it was severely hampered. The problematic events were:

a) Bushell and the escape committee agreed to proceed with the escape when the chief ferret took a two-week leave

b) Bushell continued with the escape even after the tunnel was found to be too short (see E3.24.22 in Table A.1)

c) Key members of the escape committee (decision makers) left the tunnel early (see E3.24.23 in Table A.1)

d) Escape was severely hampered by a series of

arising problems (see E3.24 to E3.25 in Table A.1)

e)   A misunderstanding over the exit signal led to the discovery of the escape and the sounding of an alarm (see E3.25.5 in Table A.1)

For contributing factor 3 (the majority of POWs [with the exception of fifteen] were poorly equipped for difficult conditions), the problematic events were:

a)   Unfavorable weather, as on the 24th snow was still on the ground

b)   The alarm was raised at 5 a.m., far earlier than the expected 8 a.m. (see E3.25.5 in Table A.1)

c)   At the highest level of alert, there were many searchers and everybody was scrutinised (see E3.25.8 in Table A.1)

Analysis Step

Why did the escape (project) go wrong? What were the contributing factors? What were the root causes of the contributing factors? For this step, you need to perform the following procedures:

- Categorise the events in priority order.

   – For contributing factor 1: c

   – For contributing factor 2: a, b, c, d

   – For contributing factor 3: a, b, c

- Analyse the root causes of the events.

The next procedure is a detailed analysis of the root causes of supporting events for contributing factor 1 (enemy tolerance for escapers was very low):

- Germany had enemies on all sides.

  - The Kommandant, being truly concerned for his own life and the lives of his men and the prisoners, addressed the POWs to explain that escape was not a game anymore and would result in executions. Notices of the Kugel order were posted in the camp.

  - Guards and ferrets increased the number and length of searches.

- Public fury over airmen (perceived as terrorists) escalated.

  - Air attacks on German cities made civilians hostile and unfriendly to escapers.

  - When Allied airmen were forced to land in Germany, the civilian population retaliated by beating, lynching, and murdering captured flyers. Often the airmen were forced to run the gauntlet whilst being attacked with shovels, clubs, and whatever was available. The police had orders not to protect the airmen and not to punish civilians for lynching them.

The detailed analysis for contributing factor 2 (the escape committee pressed on with the plan despite mounting problems):

- The escape committee met and agreed to proceed, paranoid that the tunnel would be found because of increased ferret activity.

  - They needed a moonless night, but the next window in April was too far away as the risk of discovery was very high.

- Bushell and the escape committee agreed that there would be a negative impact on morale if the escape were postponed. This is a testament to the project planning, as this scenario had been envisioned.

- The escape committee comprised seasoned escapers desperate to get out (borderline wire happy).

- Bushell agreed to continue with the escape even after the tunnel was found to be too short.

- Key members of the escape committee (decision makers) left early, having earned high priority in the queue.

- The escape was severely hampered by arising problems. The rate of escape was far slower than expected because of problems with:

  - Frozen exit

  - Luggage (suitcases) too large, blanket rolls too long

    – Air raid, resulting in lights out

    – Tunnel collapse

The detailed analysis for contributing factor 3 (the POWs were poorly equipped for difficult conditions):

- The overall track record of the escapees was poor, so the chances were low for hardarsers with limited disguises and language skills.

- Snow on the ground impeded travel and clothing was inadequate for travel on foot.

- There was an increase in the number of searchers with an earlier-than-expected alarm.

- There was an increase in the frequency of stop-checks on trains and roads when the scale of the escape was discovered and the highest level of alert was issued.

- The POWs were unable to change tactics once outside.

Corrective Actions Step

What actions can be taken to improve the chances of success for future projects? For this step, you need to perform the following procedures:

- Identify corrective actions for the root causes

- Evaluate the organisation's best practices for projects

- Implement the changes

The Corrective Actions Step tests and rationalises the root causes into true causes and determines solutions or corrective actions. The purpose of this step is to prevent the outcome from happening again.

For example, for contributing factor 1 (enemy tolerance for escapers was very low), the root causes were:

1. Higher German authorities would not tolerate a disturbance or any internal chaos that would divert resources from the war effort, especially the use of troops in a hunt for escaped POWs.

2. Camp authorities were also fearful of an escape as it would affect their own personal situations, resulting in their being posted to the eastern front or even facing the Gestapo

Root cause 1 is likely the true cause. A mass breakout was going to raise a stink at such a paranoid time. A high-risk remedy could have been to limit the number of escapees that night and create the impression that an escape took place via a different escape route, such as through the wire. This would preserve the tunnel for further escapes. However, there were great pressures to get everyone out at the next opportunity, and this urgency overshadowed the need for taking a more strategic and clandestine approach.

For contributing factor 2 (the escape committee pressed on with the plan despite mounting problems), the root causes were:

1. The poor track record of escapees on previous attempts in the camp, because of the relatively poor level of organisation, spurred the escape committee onward.

2. The escape committee comprised of seasoned escapers desperate to get out (bordering on wire happy) who dismissed the seriousness of the situation and ignored warnings from the Kommandant.

3. There were pressures to feel like part of the war effort and contribute to the Allied victory by tying down enemy resources. Bushell wanted a mass escape.

4. In project planning, the escape committee devised a contingency plan to fall back on if a tunnel was discovered. When this actually happened, they were able to switch over and continue.

5. Once the escape started, there was no turning back as there was no back-out plan, and the escape committee had not carefully thought out all the possible scenarios. If problems arose, the best that could be done was on-the-spot improvisation, which is how the project took shape to date. The escape committee chose to just get over the problem without looking too far ahead, and this was detrimental to the whole escape.

6. The ability to communicate messages to the POWs as they were going through the tunnel was very poor.

Root causes 2, 3, and 5 are likely the true causes. When the project should have shut down, upon the discovery of Tom, the escape committee resurrected it against all odds, thereby giving themselves a chance of success. This established a mindset of determination that nothing would stop them in their escape attempt.

In a critical situation, it is easy to lose control and make rash decisions based on too little information. A remedy would have been for the escape committee to follow laid-out project processes, carefully assess the risk, and make the appropriate decisions at decision points.

For contributing factor 3 (the POWs were poorly equipped for difficult conditions), the root causes were:

1. Resources did not stretch far enough to provide clothing for all two hundred and twenty escapers and so the hardarsers had little chance of success.

2. Poor weather, with snow on the ground, reduced the ability to bivouac. This made cross-country trekking next to impossible, as the snow was too wet and deep.

3. The early alarm dramatically increased the frequency of stop-checks on trains and roads, as well as the overall number of searchers. With only one rail station at Sagan, getting away became very difficult.

4. Escapees were challenged to communicate in foreign languages to maintain a disguise. It was incredibly difficult to imitate a local dialect and maintain a deception when the listener was looking for any giveaways.

Root cause 3 is likely the true cause. A remedy could have been to establish an outcome-recovery plan, carefully thought out for all possible scenarios. The plan would have had to be well communicated and regularly practiced.

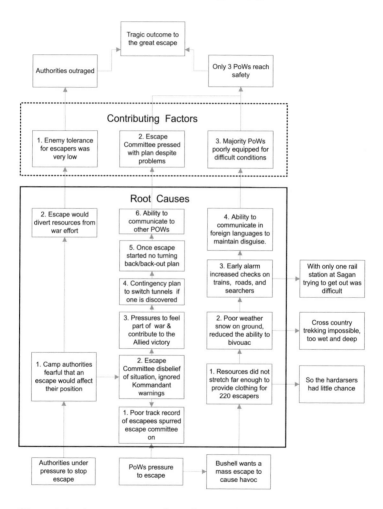

Figure 8.4: A root-cause precedence diagram shows some of the root causes that gave rise to multiple contributing factors in the escape project.

What Lessons Can Be Taken Away?

The major lessons learned regarding the positives from the project were:

- The project approach was very logical with systematic planning.

- The project was simplified by setting up numerous departments across the project to the extent that the team was able to build several tunnels and still see multiple escape attempts in this period.

- Based on extensive experience in previous escape attempts, the escape committee was able to manage the project through daily meetings.

- With limited material resources available, everything (including Red Cross parcel materials) was saved and recycled.

- The organisation was decentralised, yet six hundred men were engaged in the project. In fact, this was a high-performance team that was absolutely committed to a common cause.

- The ad hoc project team had very varied talents and showed strength in its diversity.

- All the problems were meticulously understood.

- Most problems were solved, some very ingeniously, and continuous innovation was a key trait of the project.

- An extraordinarily difficult (if not impossible) task was accomplished under very adverse circumstances.

The major lessons learned regarding the negatives from the project were:

- There was too much focus on the tunnel and its construction.

- The project team members were the beneficiaries of the project, which clouded a better sense of judgement, and priority was given to the greatest contributors to the tunnel's construction.

- There was no possibility of rerunning the escape, as the tunnel was not created for reuse. The escape had a very poor ROI, with a massive resource investment.

- Too many risks were taken in implementation. Was March the best month for escape? How could so many escapers fail to draw attention?

- There was no contingency plan to fall back on when the implementation started to go wrong, as when the tunnel was found to be too short and the air raid cut power to the tunnel. Once the escape had started, there was no stopping it.

- There was no contingency plan for concealing documents and rations left over from the escape. These ended up being destroyed and months of work were wasted. Precious resources that took months to create were irretrievably lost.

- When the tunnel was found to be too short, emotion took over, so escapers in a high state of anxiety didn't stop to reevaluate the situation and back out of the plan.

So in summary, it seemed like a perfect project, but was it? The project objectives appeared very clear at the outset, but they were unclear in hindsight.

Conclusions

In closing a project, it is important to determine whether it was a success or a failure, or in other words to assess how well it met its initial objectives. If it is considered a failure, it is especially important to go through a postmortem, but this should be done either way regardless of success to extract learning lessons and understanding for use in future projects.

CHAPTER NINE

Evaluating the PMBoK™ Knowledge Areas

"It shocked us at the time, not so much the loss of life, but how it occurred. If those chaps had actually been mown down by a guard under machine gun as they ran, we possibly would accept it. But to line them up against a wall and just give the old, you know, the Genickschuss, I mean, that's, that was something different. That's not, that's not playing it by the rules."
Former POW Jack Lyon, 2004[5]

Although the nine PMBOK™ knowledge areas were not recognised in 1944, it is interesting how well the project mapped to these principles and how their respective issues were addressed. Table 9.1 below summarises these knowledge areas and assesses how well they were applied through a score (High/Medium/Low).

Table 9.1: Summary of PMBoK knowledge areas and their application in The Great Escape		
Knowledge Area	*Description*	*Score*
Integration Management	Overall the plan was complex and difficult to execute. The full set of knowledge areas was addressed and well covered.	H
Scope Management	Great scope planning in laying out a strategy for 3 tunnels. Scope was well managed throughout the project, although a contingency plan for implementation was not completed.	M
Time Management	Sequencing of activities was critical, and this was intuitively laid out. At no point was there a major delay in the project.	M
Cost Management	A meagre budget (bribes) required ingenious resourcefulness to run the project making best use of all available resources.	H
Quality Management	Quality was ingrained into the project from the scrutiny of forged documents to clothing to tunnel construction.	H
Human Resource Management	Probably the most challenging knowledge area because of the scale of organising so many POWs (600). Once profiled for trades and skills, they were allocated to departments.	H

Communications Management	Communication was critical in informing POWs of the escape and taking all precautions to keep it secret. However, it was not at all effective in the escape itself.	L
Risk Management	Experience and knowledge in escaping was pooled to mitigate risks. Risks had to be identified, analysed, and managed. However, substantial risks were taken in the implementation itself.	L
Procurement Management	Liberating (stealing) resources, being resourceful and self-sufficient, and the ability to negotiate with (blackmail) the guards.	H

Risk Checklist for Projects

Identifying and managing risk is a critical part of projects and this procedure was performed in the Great Escape, although not through a formal process. Table 9.2 shows how the processes were acted on with actions.

In summary, when assessing the risks the escape committee understood the problems well, but some risks were missed, such as the length of the tunnel being too short and the risks that materialised in the implementation due to non-identification.

Some Best Practices

Project managers have to deal with complex multi-organisational projects that may have to be continually juggled. However, the project manager must focus on making things simple as the project moves forward.

Table 9.2: Summary of the processes in a risk checklist and the actions taken by the escape committee to address them

Process	*Actions Taken*
Establish the risk process	Although doing so only informally through the project, the escape committee was intuitively following a risk process. Evidence of this lies in some of the proactive decisions made (3-tunnel design).
Identify risks	The escape committee had several years of experience in escaping from camps, which helped in identifying risks like the contingency plan for the discovery of a single tunnel. Most aspects of the project were scrutinised for risk in 2 areas: - Escape plot discovery - Dangers with tunnel engineering
Analyse risks	Problems were well understood and methodically analysed, yet some were completely missed, like the length of the tunnel (too short), and too little attention was paid to the implementation.
Mitigate risks	Various ingenious solutions were applied throughout the construction of the 3 tunnels. Typically, these were introduced at a departmental level.
Manage risks	Well managed, with the ability to switch tunnels and utilise available resources. The escape committee kept on top of these through daily meetings.
Monitor risks	Project fell flat in the implementation as new, emerging risks were ignored and not managed.

Conclusions

What the POWs achieved was quite remarkable considering the adverse conditions under which they were operating. The POWs were driven by determination, and nothing was thought impossible. They found a way of not only initiating the project but also supporting it. The approach was one of continuous improvisation and improvement, as lessons and experience from one tunnel were transferred to the next. The prisoners devised a way around a seemingly hopeless situation and all of the many problems they encountered. They found resources in unexpected places and were able to maximise their usage and effect. The captives organised themselves so well that in some ways they became more powerful than their captors. Hampered by the continuously changing environment and unexpected daily situations, they became incredibly adept at adapting. This adaptability was to prove to be the most significant strength of the project.

In today's world, the perspectives are different and projects collect metrics to measure their success. The fact that only three POWs made it home and the remaining men were all recaptured would indicate that the project was not a true success. But the perspective was different in 1944, and Sydney Dowse, one of the few surviving Great Escapers, summed up the POWs' attitudes best when he said this in March 2004:

> "We could have just sat there and enjoyed our lives there but I do not think many of us wanted to do that. . . . Freedom, just freedom. Even if we did not get to England we were free for a few days, or a week or two and it was something to do and a lot of fun."[5]

The Great Escape was a shining example of what humanity can achieve under the most strenuous of circumstances. The resourceful POWs, using only their wits and the few materials available to them, devised and executed a brilliant plan.

Today's sensibilities and risk aversion would probably not allow the institution of such a project, although this is a futile comparison considering what POWs had to go through in prison camps. Today many projects never get off the ground for fear of failure, and the principal lesson to learn is not to let the word "no" defeat you from the outset.

CHAPTER TEN

Epilogue

In the Second World War there were 135,000 British and 95,532 US POWs taken captive in Europe. Around 180,000 Allied airmen were shot down over enemy territory. Of some 10,000 RAF POWs, only 30 of these escaped to Britain or a neutral country. Almost 36,000 Army Air Forces (AAF) personnel were confined in POW camps. Only 17 percent of POWs died in German prison camps, a much lower percentage than the death rate in Japanese camps, generally assessed in the range of 20 to 35 percent. After the Great Escape in 1944, escapes became more dangerous and yet, amazingly, attempts still continued. Prisoners who were neither British nor American had a tough time, as the Nazis did not give them the same respect and they were likely to be shot.

Transferring to Stalag VIIA

On January 27, 1945 Adolf Hitler issued an order to evacuate Stalag Luft III, as he was fearful that the Russians, who were within 20 kilometers of the camp, would liberate the 11,000 POWs being held there. The prisoners could hear the Russian artillery and see their spotter planes, and they were looking forward to liberation. However, Hitler wanted to keep the Allied airmen as hostages, and the POWs were given only thirty minutes to be at the front gate and to move out.

Figure 10.1: Forced march from Stalag Luft III.

After a grueling two-day slog, they were jammed into train boxcars, with over 100 men in each car, and shipped to Moosburg or Stalag VIIA.

Figure 10.2: Journey by train boxcars.

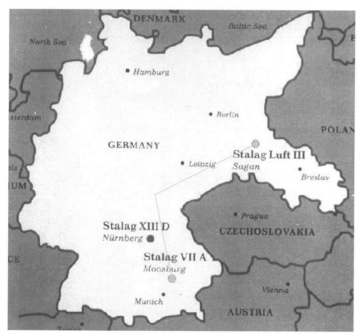

Figure 10.3: Route map for Stalag Luft III to Stalag VIIA.

215

This camp had been built to hold 14,000 French prisoners, but at this point it held 130,000 POWs of all nationalities and ranks. Five hundred POWs were crammed into a hut originally intended for an uncomfortable 200.

Figure 10.4: Guard Tower at the main entrance to Stalag VIIA.

Figure 10.5: Terrible overcrowded conditions in Stalag VIIA.

Liberation

On April 29, 1945 elements of the 14th Armored Division of Patton's 3rd Army attacked the SS troops guarding Stalag VIIA, and the POWs scrambled for safety. Eventually the invading forces broke through and the first tank entered. The POWs went wild and climbed onto the tanks.

Figure 10.6: Liberation of POWs

Initially all support of the camp stopped. The Germans who ran Stalag VIIA had all been taken off to prison camps, and there was a serious delay before a US Army support battalion was pulled out of the line to provide all necessary support for the camp. Many POWs had a dreadful experience in the last four months of the war as they were marched or transported as far as possible from advancing Allied forces.

After the Second World War, the RAF Special Investigation Branch continued to track down former Gestapo personnel and bring them to justice to face war crime tribunals for the murder of the fifty Great Escape prisoners who were recaptured. This went on for many years with some Gestapo escaping prosecution until as late as May 1968, but most of those responsible for these murders were eventually hunted down.

Remains of Stalag Luft III

Stalag Luft III was located in eastern Germany, and its remains are in what we now call Poland. In 1965 some POWs returned and couldn't find any trace of the camp at all. In 1994 further veterans visited it and they discovered that the local road showed a shallow depression running at right angles across it. This was exactly where Harry ran, 30 feet beneath, and subsidence had caused the depression to occur. Today there are very few traces of the camp left, as most of it is overgrown with forest. In 2004 archaeologists located the remains of the camp by picking out landmarks, and they discovered the foundations of the water tank, Hut 104, and the path of the tunnel. Following extensive excavation of the tunnel, they were able to recover some of the ingenious devices made by the POWs.

Great Escape Memorial Project

On the 60th Anniversary of the Great Escape in March 2004, the town of Sagan unveiled a marker to commemorate the future site of the Great Escape monument. At this event, Mayor Slawomir Kowal gave written support to proceed with the project. Polish officials agreed to donate the five acres of land and officially designate it for the establishment of the Great Escape Memorial Project, a peace development on the site with a memorial, a meditation garden, and a park.[12]

Figure 10.7: At the 60th Anniversary tribute, Polish soldiers stand by Harry.

Timeline of Significant Events

Table A.1: Event timeline for The Great Escape			
Event ID	*Date*	*Event*	*Description*
	1943		
D1.1	Many	Public disturbances with Allied airmen landing in Germany	Civilians turn nasty and attack captured airmen
D3.1	Mar 1943	Building the North Compound.	A select group of POWs (escape committee) help finish it off

Event ID	Date	Event	Description
D4.23	23 Apr	Transfer of POWs to the North Compound	Up to 600 POWs make the move
D5.31	End of May	Traps are finished for all 3 tunnels	Tunneling begins in earnest as tunnel shafts are dropped from the traps
D6.1	Early Jun	"Harry" and "Dick" are suspended and sealed	Efforts concentrate on "Tom"
D6.3	3 Jun	As the tunnels reach 20 feet (6 meters) the railway system is created	It is critical to improving the efficiency of the operation
D6.8	8 Jun	Authorities start to build a new camp to the south for American POWs	Efforts increase on Tom to allow American POWs to escape
D7.4	4 Jul	Independence Day celebrations	American POWs throw a party to raise morale
D7.15	Mid Jul	Sand is put down Dick	Makeshift location as other options for sand dispersal are reduced

Event ID	Date	Event	Description
D9.8	8 Sep	Tom is discovered	Major turmoil in the camp
D9.15	Mid Sep	Harry and Dick are sealed up	Tunneling is given a low priority to prevent further discovery
	1944		
E1.8	8 Jan	Work resumes on Harry	Tunnel is reopened
E2.10	10 Feb	Progress on Harry is rapid	Second halfway house is added
E2.28	End of Feb	"Stfe Roemisch III Order" is issued	Every escaped officer POW, other than British or American, is handed over to the Gestapo
E3.1	Early Mar	"Kugel Order" (bullet decree) is issued	The immediate execution of any escapers found on the ground
E3.15	Mar 15	Tunnel (Harry) is ready	Less than 1 foot of sand had to be dug out of the exit shaft on the escape night
E3.23	Mar 23	The next possible moonless nights.	A requirement for a successful escape

Event ID	Date	Event	Description
E3.24-.11:30	Mar 24	11:30 a.m. decision to proceed	Bushell makes the final decision
E3.24-.21:30	Mar 24	9:30 p.m. zero hour and escape starts	Problems with opening up the exit, frozen into place
E3.24-.22	Mar 24	10:00 p.m. tunnel found to be too short	Tunnel is 20 feet (6 meters) short but decision is made to continue
E3.24-.22:30	Mar 24	10:30 p.m. escapers move out	Escapers leave the tunnel using a signaling system
E3.24-.23:45	Mar 24	11:45 p.m. lights go out	Air raid over Berlin forces blackout
E3.25-.1	Mar 25	1:00 a.m. first group through	Suitcase carriers are through and at Sagan station
E3.25-.1:30	Mar 25	1:30 a.m. escaper comes off the trolley	In fixing it, 3 feet (1 meter) of the roof collapses and needs repair
E3.25-.2:30	Mar 25	2:30 a.m. decision made to put through only 100 escapers, as not enough time	Escapers number 100 to 200 have to abandon the escape

Event ID	Date	Event	Description
E3.25-.4:55	Mar 25	4:55 a.m. guard answers call of nature	Uncovers escape and alarm is set off
E.31	Late Mar	Peter Bergsland and Jens Müller make it to Sweden	Traveled through Germany from Frankfurt to Stettin
E7.8	Jul 8	Van Stock makes it to Gibraltar and earns a home run	Traveled through Germany, Holland, France, and Spain

The Ones that Got Away

Of the hundreds of POWs who worked so hard to make the Great Escape possible, only three made it to freedom and scored a winning "home run." In the following accounts, Alan Burgess[13] shares the personal stories of the three lucky men who beat all the odds.

Sergeant Peter Bergsland and Lieutenant Jens Müller

Sergeant Peter Bergsland was Norwegian. When the Germans invaded his country he fled to England. There he joined the RAF, was shot down, and duly arrived at Stalag Luft III.

Sergeant Bergsland and his partner, fellow countryman Lieutenant Jens Müller, also with the RAF, decided to team up for the Sagan escape. They headed for Stettin, where Swedish ships regularly docked and departed. Both spoke perfect Swedish.

Figure B.1: In this photo from Stalag Luft III, Peter Bergsland (left) and Jens Müller (right) pose prior to the Great Escape with fellow Norwegian Halldor Espelid, who was caught after the break and executed.

They came out of the tunnel as Numbers 43 and 44, and Müller was surprised at the ease of passage through Harry. His report to Intelligence explained what had happened: "It took me three minutes to get through the tunnel. Above ground I crawled along holding the rope for several feet; it was tied to a tree. Sergeant Bergsland joined me; we arranged our clothes and walked to the Sagan railway station.

"Bergsland was wearing a civilian suit he had made for himself from a Royal Marine uniform, with an RAF overcoat slightly altered with brown leather sewn over the buttons. A black RAF tie, no hat. He carried a small suitcase that had been sent from Norway. In it were Norwegian toothpaste and soap, sandwiches, and 163 reichsmarks given to him by the escape committee.

"We caught the 2:04 train to Frankfurt an der Oder. Our papers stated that we were Norwegian electricians from the Arbeitslager [labor camp] in Frankfurt working in the vicinity of Sagan. For the journey from Frankfurt to Stettin we had other papers ordering us to change our place of work from Frankfurt to Stettin, and to report to the Bürgermeister of Stettin."

They were now inside the docks, and they had to get out. The journey was uneventful. They traveled in a third-class carriage full of civilians and looked like any ordinary travelers. They arrived at Frankfurt at 6:00 in the morning and caught a connecting train to Küstrin at 8:00 a.m. They had a beer in the station cafe, and while they were sipping, the first inspection took place. A wandering German *Feldwebel* [sergeant] of the military police approached them. He looked at the cheerful, fresh-faced young men who spoke excellent German with a Norwegian accent, gave their papers a cursory examination, touched his cap, and departed. Bergsland and Müller clinked mugs, smiled, and drank up.

They caught the 10:00 a.m. train from Küstrin to Stettin and arrived at lunchtime.

"We walked around the town, visited a cinema and a beer hall, and after dusk went to an address given to us by the escape committee.

"It was a French brothel bearing the inscription, 'Nur fur Ausländers—Deutschen verboten' ['Only for foreigners—Germans forbidden']. We knocked on the door. As we did so a Pole who was standing on the street approached us and asked us if we had any black-market wares for sale. We asked him if he knew any Swedish sailors. He fetched one out of the brothel. We made our identity known, talking in Swedish, and he told us that his ship was leaving that night and to meet us at 20:00 hours outside the brothel."

The Swede was as good as his word, and was waiting for them when they returned. He led them to the docks and told them to duck under a chain while he reported to the Control Office. He would then go aboard, wait for an all-clear, and then whistle them to come aboard.

They waited in vain. No signal was given. Seamen cast off the ropes and they watched the ship set sail down the channel. They could hazard a guess that the sailor had probably tried to enlist help to get them aboard only to be told by his friends that one was likely to end up in a Nazi concentration camp if caught. They were now inside the docks, and they had to get out. The best meeting place in town was obviously the brothel, if they could get through. They decided to take a chance, and the officer at Control hardly bothered to glance at their papers. Disappointingly, though, the brothel was a no-nonsense establishment and closed its doors at 2:00 a.m.

The area itself, however, was certainly populated by seamen, and they looked like seamen. Small cafes were open and small, sordid hotels did business. They had a meal and paid for a room in one of the hotels. They had participated in one of the most momentous escapes in history; they'd taken their chances and got away with it. They were already asleep as their heads fell towards the pillows, and they did not wake until four o'clock the following afternoon. Müller looked across at Bergsland and grinned. "Another visit to 17 Klein Oder Strasse, I think."

They arrived at the brothel at six and met two more Swedish sailors coming out through the door. The seamen were affable when the two Norwegians explained their difficulties.

"Ja," they said. "You come, catch the tram with us and we go back to our docks. Four miles out near Parnitz." By that time it was 8:30 and getting dark. The Swedish sailors slouched up to the German soldier on guard, showing their papers, the two Norwegians close behind. The guard was helpful. "All part of the same crew?" he inquired, and Bergsland and Müller nodded vigorously. He stood aside to let them pass, not even asking them for papers.

Once the Norwegians were safely on deck, the Swedes slapped them on the back and one of them said, "Not bad, eh? Now we've got to hide you because the ship doesn't sail until seven tomorrow morning, and there's bound to be a German search before we sail."

Their hiding place was the anchor locker holding the great coiled chain. In one corner was a pile of netting and sacks. The sailors heaved it aside and formed a sort of inner nest. "Now you can sleep. But don't be snoring when the Germans arrive tomorrow morning. Usually they don't have dogs. Dogs don't like climbing up and down thin steel companion ladders."

Hours later Bergsland and Müller heard the Germans tramping towards them. The hatch was thrown open and closed again; the search was perfunctory. The feet stamped away. Half an hour later the propellers began to thrash water and they felt the ship begin to move. Their two friends came down with food and drink, and the smell of the sea coming in through the hawseholes in the bow was like an elixir of freedom. When they reached Sweden they shook hands and gave a whoop for joy, for it was a small victory for them. Then they went to find the British consulate. Two out of the seventy-six had reached freedom.

Flight Lieutenant Bram van der Stok

[Van der Stok] had managed to get out of Holland when the Nazis invaded, and [he] had flown with the RAF during those first months of the war. Because of his zeal for escaping, his intelligence, his familiarity with the countryside, and his gift for languages, the escape committee [formed by POWs at Stalag Luft III] had rated his chances of making a home run very highly, and he was among the first twenty through the tunnel. He was traveling alone. Cautiously he made his way through the woods and almost bumped into a dark figure. It was a

Figure B.2: Bram van der Stok in his RAF uniform.

German civilian who said sharply, "What are you doing in these woods at this time of night?"

Van der Stok had rehearsed his reply to that question. "I'm a Dutch worker. I'm afraid the police might arrest me for being out of doors during an air raid. Do you speak Dutch? I'm a bit scared."

The German did not speak Dutch, but van der Stok's cover was perfect and the civilian took him under his wing. "I know the way to the station. You stick with me and you'll be all right."

At the station the German left van der Stok to his own devices, and the first thing the escaper discovered was that the heavy raid on Berlin had delayed his train by three hours. The Dutchman wished someone could have told the chief of Bomber Command what trouble he was causing his fellow air force men. He then observed one of the German censors at the camp. He knew her slightly by sight; he hoped to God she didn't know him. But she was suspicious of one of the men on the platform, whom van der Stok recognised as Thomas Kirby-Green [a British pilot who was later recaptured at Hodonin in Czechoslovakia and shot on March 29]. If the police picked him up they would be alerted at once. He hardly dared look around—the station was full of Stalag Luft III escapers.

He saw eight fellow escapers from Sagan, but not even by the flutter of an eyebrow did he offer a sign of recognition. And—oh, hell—she was telling an officer of the German military police to go accost Kirby-Green and demand to see his papers. Then he became conscious that the bright female eyes were fixed on him. Bram van der Stok moved closer, not farther away. The only way to counter suspicion was to face it. One thing the escape committee had not taken into consideration was a female Sherlock Holmes sitting in the Sagan station. Her question was abrupt.

"You are traveling tonight?"

At least he was comfortable with his German. "Yes, I'm Dutch—you can probably tell from my accent."

"You know the trains are running late?"

"Yes, I understand that is so." Van der Stok gave a quick glance at Kirby-Green, who was putting his papers away. The military policeman was satisfied. Thank God for that.

"There are many strangers around these days," said the Dutchman equably. That seemed to satisfy her. She had done her duty as a good German woman.

The train for Breslau arrived at 3:30 a.m. Bram van der Stok traveled second-class. He saw eight fellow escapers from Sagan, among them Roger Bushell and Bernard Scheidhauer, but not even by the slightest change in expression did he betray this recognition. They chugged into Breslau station at 5:00 a.m. There was no bustle of security, no groups of Gestapo or military police with hard watchful eyes. The tunnel hadn't been discovered ... yet!

Bram van der Stok sat on a bench in the Breslau railway station and pretended to doze. He believed in the sentiment, "He travels fastest who travels alone." He was wearing civilian clothes—at least they looked like that, although they were in fact an Australian air force overcoat and a converted naval jacket and trousers, RAF shoes, and a beret.

He bought a second-class ticket to Alkmaar, boarded the train, and at 10:00 a.m. arrived in Dresden, where he had a long layover. He dozed in two cinemas until 8:00 p.m., then went back to the station to catch a train to the Dutch border at Bentheim. He realised that the tunnel had been discovered and the hunt was on, because his papers were carefully scrutinised on four occasions. At the frontier post his papers were examined again, but now it was easier. His Dutch was, naturally, perfect, and his papers were in order.

He traveled by train to Oldenzaal, then on to Utrecht. There he found an underground resistance worker through an address that the escape committee had given him. The man welcomed him, gave him fake identity papers and ration cards, and kept him safe in his home for three days. But there was no victory yet. Holland was part of Germany's conquered Europe; informers and spies were everywhere. Bram van der Stok still had to move fast.

He traveled by bicycle to another safe house in Belgium where he was given Belgian identity papers, then on by train through Brussels and Paris. More false papers and south again to Toulouse, and now he was installed in the Maquis resistance chain [the French resistance]. He met up with two American lieutenants, two RAF pilots, a French officer, a Russian, and a French girl who acted as a guide. Together they crossed the Pyrenees and arrived in Lérida. The Spanish were neutral but not necessarily friendly. The British Consul took them over in Lérida, and Bram van der Stok arrived in Gibraltar on July 8.

His escape journey had taken almost three and a half months. He was back in England within a few days, the third to make a home run.

Notes and References

1. "World War Two: The Great Escape." *History on the Net.*
    History on the Net. 2000-2005. Updated 5 Nov. 2005. 31
    Mar. 2006. <http://www.historyonthenet.com/WW2/
    great_escape.htm>

2. Dove, Rick. "Decision Making, Value Propositioning, and
    Project Failures - Reality and Responsibility." *Proceedings of
    the International Council on Systems Engineering (INCOSE)
    2004 Region II Conference, Sept 2004.* Rpt. In *Projects and
    Profits.* Jan. 2005. <http://icfaipress.org/105/
    pp.asp?mag=http://www.icfaipress.
    org/105/pp_sub.asp>

3. "Lancaster Avro 1." *Royal Air Force Museum Collection.*
    Collection Ref. 74/A/12. Trustees of the Royal Air Force
    Museum, 2002. 31 Mar. 2006. <http://www.
    rafmuseum.org.uk/avro-lancaster-1.htm>

4. Carroll, Tim. *The Great Escape from Stalag Luft III: The Full Story of How 76 Allied Officers Carried Out World War II's Most Remarkable Mass Escape.* New York: Pocket Books, Aug. 2005. Excerpt in simonsays.com. Simon & Schuster, Inc. 29 Mar. 2006. <http://www.simonsays.com/content/book.cfm?sid=33&pid=508729&agid=2>

5. Burgess, Alan. *The Longest Tunnel: The True Story of World War II's Great Escape.* New York: Naval Institute Press, 2004.

6. This is known as the Reverse Stockholm Syndrome, a psychological response observed in prolonged, emotionally charged captor/captive situations in which captors sympathise with their captives and exhibit seeming loyalty to them in spite of the danger.

7. The Project Management Body of Knowledge (PMBOK) is a collection of processes and knowledge areas generally accepted as a best practice within the project management discipline. PMBOK is a trademark of the Project Management Institute, Inc. which is registered in the United States of America and other nations. "PMBOK Guide Third Edition Excerpts." *Product Excerpts > Standards Overview.* Project Management Institute, Inc. 2005. 31 Mar. 2006. <http://www.pmi.org/info/pp_pmbok2000welcome.asp>

8. Gill, Anton. *The Great Escape: The Full Dramatic Story with Contributions from Survivors and Their Families.* London: Headline Review, 2002.

9. Hickman, Mark. "Squadron Leader Roger Joyce Bushell < Biographies." *Prisoner of War.* 6 Jan. 2002. 31 Mar. 2006. <http://www.pegasus-one.org/pow/roger_bushell.htm>

10. James, Jimmy. *The Great Escape in the Words of Jimmy James – Part Two.* Edited transcript. BBC Radio Shropshire. 2000. 31 Mar. 2006. <http://www.bbc.co.uk/shropshire/history/2004/03/great_escape_06.shtml>

11. The Geneva Convention of 1929 dictated that servicemen out of uniform could be shot as spies.

12. "Background Information." *The Great Escape Memorial Project.* The International Great Escape Memorial Committee. 2006. 31 Mar. 2006. <http://www.thegreatescapememorialproject.com/>

13. Burgess, Alan. "The Three That Got Away < Great Escape." *Great Escape.* WGBH Educational Foundation for PBS Online. 1996-2004. 29 Mar. 2006. <http://www.pbs.org/wgbh/nova/greatescape/three.html>

The following work was used as a source throughout this book:

Brickhill, Paul. *The Great Escape.* New York: Amereone Ltd., 1950.

Photo Credits

- Front cover: HU21190. POWs disguised in German uniforms. Used with permission from the Imperial War Museum, London. <http://london.iwm.org.uk/upload/package/40/GreatEscapes/about4.htm>.

- Front cover: HU21013. The Prisoner of War camp at Stalag Lüft III, general view of the huts and compound. Used with permission from the Imperial War Museum, London. <http://www.pegasus-one.org/pow/main.htm>.

- Figure 1.1: Lancaster. History of Aviation website. <http://history.sandiego.edu/gen/st/~jgaffney/aviation/images/ww2/lancaster.jpg>.

- The following photos and diagrams are used with the

permission of the United States Air Force Academy museum. <http://afhi.org/museum/stalag/about.html>. These materials reside in the U.S. Air Force Academy Library's Special Collections:

- Figures 1.2 to 1.7
- Figures 2.1 to 2.18
- Figures 3.2 to 3.4
- Figure 4.2
- Figures 5.2, 5.3
- Figures 6.3 to 6.6, 6.8, 6.10 to 6.18
- Figures 8.1 to 8.2
- Figure 10.1 to 10.6

- Figure 4.1: Squadron Leader Roger Bushell. Copyright: Elizabeth Carter. <http://www.pegasus-one.org/pow/SL3/PicSL_3_Bushell3.htm>.

- Figure 4.3: An aerial photo of the North Compound, showing the positions of the escape tunnels Tom, Dick, and Harry. <http://www.pegasus-one.org/pow/main.htm>.

- Smith, Mary and Barbara Freer. "The Photos > World War II Prisoner of War – Stalag Luft I: A Collection of Stories, Photos, Art and Information on Stalag Luft I." *Stalag Luft I Online*. 31 Mar. 2006. <http://www.merkki.com/photo.htm>.

- Figure A.1: "Bergsland/Espelid/Müller." Courtesy of

Jonathan Vance, University of Western Ontario.

- Figure A.2: "Bram van der Stok, Bernard Scheidhauer." Courtesy of Ian Le Seuer.

- Figure 10.7: "The Great Escape Memorial Project." *The International Great Escape Memorial Committee. 2006.* 31 Mar. 2006.

- Figures GE.1 to GE.3 Courtesy of The Great Escape Memorial Project.

Glossary

Appell	Roll call parade in morning and afternoon.
Barracks	Troop quarters.
Contact	German-speaking POW assigned to befriend a ferret.
Cooler	Solitary confinement cell for POWs to cool off in.
Duty Pilot	POW watching movement at the gate.
Ersatz	Artificial, substitute.
Ferret	Specially trained anti-escape specialist.
Flieger	Flyer, aircraft.
FOODACCO	Food Account.

Friendly/Tame Ferret Ferret who gave some degree of assistance to POWs.

Geneva Convention 1929 agreement for protection of prisoners of war.

Gestapo *Geheime Staatspolizei*, Nazi Political Police.

Goon Guard.

Hardarsers Escapees with least chance of escaping.

International Red Cross One of three neutral organisations whose representatives were permitted direct contact with POWs; the other two were the Swiss Legation in Berlin and the Swedish YMCA.

Kriege German term for prisoner of war, shortening of *Kriegsgefangener*.

Palliass A mattress consisting of a thin pad filled with straw or sawdust.

Parole Written promise of a POW to fulfill stated conditions in exchange for certain privileges; usually carried threat of death if violated.

Runner POW sent by the duty pilot to warn the stooges.

Stalag Luft Air Force permanent POW camp, from German *Stammlager Luftwaffe*.

Stooge	POW watcher/guard who followed ferrets around the camp.
Terrorflieger	Terror flyer.
Trap Fuhrer	POW who was responsible for a trap, its concealment, and its operation.
Wehrmacht	Armed forces.

Acronyms

BBC	British Broadcasting Corporation.
POW	Prisoner of War.
RAF	Royal Air Force.
RAAF	Royal Australian Air Force.
RCAF	Royal Canadian Air Force.
RNZAF	Royal New Zealand Air Force.
ROI	Return on Investment.
RSAAF	Royal South African Air Force.
SBO	Senior British Officer.
USAAF or USAAC	United States Air Force: US Army Air Forces, US Army Air Corps

About the Author

As the author behind the "Lessons from History" series, Mark Kozak-Holland brings years of experience as a consultant who helps Fortune-500 companies formulate projects that leverage emerging technologies. Since 1985 he has been straddling the business and IT worlds, making these projects happen. He is a certified business consultant, the author of several books, and a noted speaker. As a historian, Kozak-Holland seeks out the wisdom of the past to help others avoid repeating mistakes and to capture time-proven techniques. His lectures have been very popular at gatherings of project managers and CIOs.

Mark is very passionate about history and sees its potential use as an educational tool in business today. As a result, he has been developing the "Lessons from History" series for organisations, applying today's Information

Technology (IT) to common business problems. It is written for primarily business and IT professionals looking for inspiration for their projects. It uses relevant historical case studies to examine how historical projects and emerging technologies of the past solved complex problems.

For thousands of years people have been running projects that leveraged emerging technologies of the time, to create unique and wonderful structures like the pyramids, buildings, or bridges. Similarly, people have gone on great expeditions and journeys and have raced their rivals in striving to be first, e.g., circumnavigating the world or conquering the poles. These were all forms of projects that required initiation, planning and design, production, implementation, and breakout.

The series looks at historical projects and then draws comparisons to challenges encountered in today's projects. It outlines the stages involved in delivering a complex project, providing a step-by-step guide to the project deliverables. It vividly describes the crucial lessons from historical projects and complements these with some of today's best practices.

This makes the whole learning experience more memorable. The series should inspire the reader, as these historical projects were achieved with a less sophisticated emerging technology.

Email: **mark.kozak-holl@sympatico.ca**

Web Sites: **http://www.mmpubs.com/kozak-holland/**
             http://www.lessons-from-history.com/

The Great Escape Memorial Project

During the Second World War, 76 prisoners of war escaped through a 323-foot man-made tunnel from Stalag III, Luft Waffe Camp in Sagan, Germany (now Zagan, Poland). All but three of the escapees were recaptured and 50 were executed contrary to the Geneva Convention. Stalag Luft III housed over 10,000 prisoners of war from around the world.

In November 2001, Carrie Tobolski (granddaughter of Pawel Tobolski, one the 50 executed during the Great Escape) and Calgary architect, Ryan Scarff traveled to Zagan, Poland to view the site where the great escape took place and present the memorial project proposal to the Mayor, Zagan Municipal Council and the Cultural Minister. The Polish officials embraced by the memorial monument concept and the idea of preserving the historical event and educating future generations. Carrie and Ryan then returned to Zagan for the 60th Anniversary of the Great Escape. Following the trip, support was granted to pursue this project and the land was designated for this project.

The **Great Escape Memorial Project** (GEMP) was founded in November 2002 in Calgary, Alberta Canada, with a mandate to establish a memorial monument in Zagan, Poland at the site where the "Great Escape" took place. The purpose is to honor the memory of the 50 prisoners of war that were executed at Stalag Luft III and pay respect and honor all survivors of World War II prisoner of war camps. The Great Escape Memorial Project Committee consists of a volunteer twelve member Advisory Council that meets monthly and numerous volunteers and family members of Stalag Luft lll prisoners of war committed to seeing this project come to fruition. Currently our Advisory Council includes two direct prisoner of war survivors from the Stalag Luft lll Camp (Dr. George Mckiel, Dr. Vince Murphy) and four family members of Stalag Luft III prisoners of war (Mrs. Roxana Anderson (daughter of Ivan Anderson), Duncan McKillop (son of Duncan McKillop Sr.), Carrie Tobolski (granddaughter of Pawel Tobolski), Scott Gilbertson (grandson of Author William Simpson). Additional advisors include Twyla Tobler, Dick Westbury, Ryan Scarff, Matthew Chow, Dennis Anderson and Shannyn Scarff. Many prisoner of war survivors also actively participate on our sub-committees.

The mandate of the Committee is to build a memorial that will mark the entrance and exit of the man made tunnel and it is hoped, increase awareness of this historical event through education as well as serve as a location for those who lost family members and friends to grieve and find closure. The

Figure GE.1: Suggested architectural rendering of the monument marking the entrance of the tunnel.

Figure GE.2: Suggested architectural rendering marking the exit of the tunnel.

land at the Stalag Luft III Camp in Zagan Poland has been designated for this project by the Mayor of Zagan Poland.

As the Great Escape Memorial Project Advisory Committee was founded and is located in Calgary, a second memorial monument will also be placed in Calgary. This Canadian memorial monument will honor the Canadian POW Survivors and the fifty that lost their lives at the Stalag Luft Camp

On January 19, 2006, The Great Escape Memorial Project Committee hosted "The Great Escape Memorial Project Gala." This gala event took place at the Calgary Chamber of Commerce. Keynote speaker Hon. Col. Arthur Smith along with many other dignitaries attended this fundraising event. This gala sold out seven weeks in advance and garnered a lot of attention with the military, corporate and media community. Many surviving POWs from the Stalag Luft Camp, along with their friends and family, were present that evening. This event was successful in garnering much needed awareness about the Great Escape and also the memorial project as well as the financing required to commission the architectural working drawings.

In April 2006, The Great Escape Memorial Project Committee (GEMP) voted and commissioned the project architect to create the official working drawings for the design and implementation of the Calgary tribute monument. Following completion of Phase I (Calgary), and upon securing the funds required, Phase II will commence in Poland.

There is only a handful of POW survivors of Stalag Luft III alive today thus creating a sense of urgency to commence building of the project so that we can pay respect and honor all those POWs who lost their lives to this tragedy, those survivors who have passed on and the few remaining that are alive today.

By supporting this International Project, you will help...

- Honor and preserve the memory of the few remaining survivors, their families and all those who died fighting for humanity at the Stalag Luft Camp

- Contribute to a local, national and international project

- Promote cross cultural education initiatives for future generations.

- Be part of history in the making

Project Estimated Cost

We are seeking corporate and individual support in raising the $350,000 required for the memorial monuments in Calgary, Alberta, Canada and also in Zagan, Poland.

The Great Escape Memorial Project Committee will work closely with each Company, Foundation or Individual to customize a recognition package that meets the needs and objectives of each individual company community investment or sponsorship mandate.

The contribution of the corporate community and from individuals will provide a fitting and lasting tribute to honor Second World War prisoner of war who lost their lives, those survivors who have passed on and the few remaining today. All Canadian donations will be gratefully appreciated and a charitable tax receipt will be issued (in accordance with Revenue Canada guidelines).

We look forward to discussing details of this project further with you. Additional information regarding the Great Escape Memorial Project can be found on the official website at **www.thegreatescapememorialproject.com** or by calling the Great Escape Memorial Project head quarters at (403) 245-6693.

On a personal note, having been involved from the onset of this memorial initiative, I have had the great honor of meeting many of the prisoner of war survivors and listening to their stories of bravery, camaraderie and humility. Many of these industrious men have gone on not only touch the lives of their friends and family but also those lucky enough to make their acquaintance. These men were extremely intelligent and determined, many took the skills they learned during war and transferred them into a skill set that made them leaders in their career field, whether it be medical, legal, political or corporate.

One gentleman in mind that exemplifies this would be Dr. Vince Murphy a PFF navigator from WWll and POW from the Stalag Luft Camp. Dr. Murphy generously sits on our

Advisory Council. He is 84 years young, and an extremely respected Orthopedic Surgeon in Calgary Alberta who to this day goes into work three half days a week because as he told me, he has clients who have been coming to him for over many, many years and he feels a commitment to them to look after them. Dr Murphy is cherished by his wife and his multitude of family, friends and colleagues. When visiting his practice located in the heart of downtown Calgary, you can admire the sketches by Stalag Luft lll POW survivor, Lee Kenyon, that depict the story of the Great Escape, images of teamwork among the men and the grueling work that took place within the tunnels. Dr. Murphy is truly an inspiring man with an amazing story....

Over the years, we have received many phone calls, letters and emails from survivors, family and friends from around the world. It is not unusual to receive a call from Australia, the UK, South Africa, the US and so on, with words of encouragement to see the project come to fruition. People are interested in sharing with us their stories about their fathers, brothers, husband or best friend who spent time at the Stalag Luft Camp. Through our website and public awareness campaign, and medium such as this book, we are able to reach out to an international community separated only by country borders around the world.

The Great Escape Memorial Project Committee is extremely grateful to publications such as this one that educate it's readers on this significant event. It is through awareness and visibility that this inspiring and touching story will continue to be told through the generations.

A portion of the proceeds from the sale of this book is directly donated to the Great Escape Memorial Project.

Shannyn Scarff
Advisor, Fundraising &
Communications
The Great Escape Memorial Project

The "Great Escape Tunnel Martyr" Print

The following print includes the actual official identity pictures taken from the German files of the 50 men who were executed for their participation in the Great Escape The photos and images depicted in this print were researched and compiled by Mr. Myron Williams, The family of each of these 50 men were presented with this print as tribute to their loved ones. The limited edition prints were donated to the Great Escape Memorial Project in June, 2006 by the Calgary Chapter of the Prisoner of War Association. Proceeds raised from this print are dedicated to contributing to the costs of building the memorial monuments. If you are interested in purchasing a print, please visit the GEMP website at **www.thegreatescapememorialproject.com** for more details.

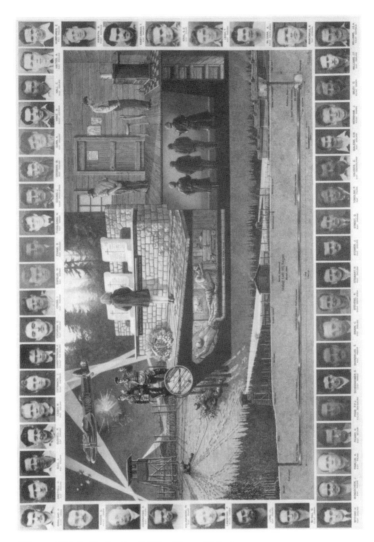

Figure GE.3: Stalag Luft III - Tunnel Martyrs.

HISTORY

About the Series

This series is for primarily business and IT professionals looking for inspiration for their projects. Specifically, business managers responsible for solving business problems, or Project Managers (PMs) responsible for delivering business solutions through IT projects.

This series uses relevant historical case studies to examine how historical projects and emerging technologies of the past solved complex problems. It then draws comparisons to challenges encountered in today's IT projects.

This series benefits the reader in several ways:

- It outlines the stages involved in delivering a complex IT project providing a step-by-step guide to the project deliverables.

- It vividly describes the crucial lessons from historical projects and complements these with some of today's best practices.

- It makes the whole learning experience more memorable.

The series should inspire the reader as these historical projects were achieved with a lesser (inferior) technology.

Website: **http://www.lessons-from-history.com/**

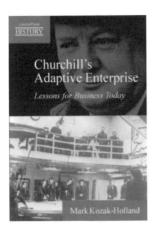

Churchill's Adaptive Enterprise: Lessons for Business Today

This book analyzes a period of time from World War II when Winston Churchill, one of history's most famous leaders, faced near defeat for the British in the face of sustained German attacks. The book describes the strategies he used to overcome incredible odds and turn the tide on the impending invasion. The historical analysis is done through a modern business and information technology lens, describing Churchill's actions and strategy using modern business tools and techniques. Aimed at business executives, IT managers, and project managers, the book extracts learnings from Churchill's experiences that can be applied to business problems today. Particular themes in the book are knowledge management, information portals, adaptive enterprises, and organizational agility.

ISBN: 1-895186-19-6   (paperback)
ISBN: 1-895186-20-X   (PDF ebook)

http://www.mmpubs.com/churchill

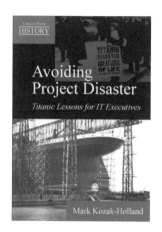

Avoiding Project Disaster: Titanic Lessons for IT Executives

Imagine you are in one of *Titanic's* lifeboats. As you look back at the wreckage site, you wonder what could have happened. What were the causes? How could things have gone so badly wrong?

Titanic's maiden voyage was a disaster waiting to happen as a result of the compromises made in the project that constructed the ship. This book explores how modern executives can take lessons from a nuts-and-bolts construction project like *Titanic* and use those lessons to ensure the right approach to developing online business solutions. Looking at this historical project as a model will prove to be incisive as it cuts away the layers of IT jargon and complexity.

Avoiding Project Disaster is about delivering IT projects in a world where being on time and on budget is not enough. You also need to be up and running around the clock for your customers and partners. This book will help you successfully maneuver through the ice floes of IT management in an industry with a notoriously high project failure rate.

ISBN: 1-895186-73-0   (paperback)
Also available in ebook formats.

http://www.mmpubs.com/disaster

Titanic Lessons for IT Projects

Titanic Lessons for IT Projects analyzes the project that designed, built, and launched the ship, showing how compromises made during early project stages led to serious flaws in this supposedly "perfect ship." In addition, the book explains how major mistakes during the early days of the ship's operations led to the disaster. All of these disasterous compromises and mistakes were fully avoidable.

Entertaining and full of intriguing historical details, this companion book to *Avoiding Project Disaster: Titanic Lessons for IT Executives* helps project managers and IT executives see the impact of decisions similar to the ones that they make every day. An easy read full of illustrations and photos to help explain the story and to help drive home some simple lessons.

ISBN: 1-895186-26-9   (paperback)
Also available in ebook formats.

http://www.mmpubs.com/titanic

Corporate Intelligence Awareness: Securing the Competitive Edge

In this compelling new book by a former diplomat, you will learn the secrets (step by step) to developing an intelligence strategy by effective information gathering and analyzing, and then to delivering credible intelligence to senior management. Along the way, you will learn how to better read people and organizations and get them to open up and share information with you—all the while behaving in an ethical, legal manner. Understanding how intelligence is gathered and processed will keep you ahead of the game, protect your secrets, and secure your competitive edge!

ISBN: 1-895186-42-0   (hardcover)
ISBN: 1-895186-43-9   (PDF ebook)

Also available in other ebook formats. Order from your local bookseller, Amazon.com, or directly from the publisher at **http://www.mmpubs.com/cia**

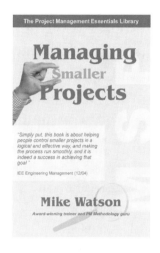

Managing Smaller Projects:
A Practical Approach

So called "small projects" can have potentially alarming consequences if they go wrong, but their control is often left to chance. The solution is to adapt tried and tested project management techniques.

This book provides a low overhead, highly practical way of looking after small projects. It covers all the essential skills: from project start-up, to managing risk, quality and change, through to controlling the project with a simple control system. It cuts through the jargon of project management and provides a framework that is as useful to those lacking formal training, as it is to those who are skilled project managers and want to control smaller projects without the burden of bureaucracy.

Read this best-selling book from the U.K., now making its North American debut. *IEE Engineering Management* praises the book, noting that "Simply put, this book is about helping people control smaller projects in a logical and effective way, and making the process run smoothly, and is indeed a success in achieving that goal."

Available in print format. Order from your local bookseller, Amazon.com, or directly from the publisher at
www.mmpubs.com/msp

Managing Agile Projects

Are you being asked to manage a project with unclear requirements, high levels of change, or a team using Extreme Programming or other Agile Methods?

If you are a project manager or team leader who is interested in learning the secrets of successfully controlling and delivering agile projects, then this is the book for you.

From learning how agile projects are different from traditional projects, to detailed guidance on a number of agile management techniques and how to introduce them onto your own projects, this book has the insider secrets from some of the industry experts – the visionaries who developed the agile methodologies in the first place.

ISBN: 1-895186-11-0   (paperback)
ISBN: 1-895186-12-9   (PDF ebook)

http://www.agilesecrets.com

By Peter R. Garber

Want to Get Ahead in Your Career?

Do you find yourself challenged by office politics, bad things happen-ing to good careers, dealing with the "big cheeses" at work, the need for effective networking skills, and keeping good working relation-ships with coworkers and bosses? *Winning the Rat Race at Work* is a unique book that provides you with case studies, interactive exercises, self-assessments, strategies, evaluations, and models for overcoming these workplace challenges. The book illustrates the stages of a career and the career choices that determine your future, empowering you to make positive changes.

Written by Peter R. Garber, the author of *100 Ways to Get on the Wrong Side of Your Boss*, this book is a must read for anyone interested in getting ahead in his or her career. You will want to keep a copy in your top desk drawer for ready reference whenever you find yourself in a challenging predicament at work.

ISBN: 1-895186-68-4   (paperback)
Also available in ebook formats. Order from your local bookseller, Amazon.com, or directly from the publisher at
http://www.mmpubs.com/rats

100 Ways to Get on the
Wrong Side
of your Boss

And
Strategies
to Prevent
you from
Getting There !

Author of Winning the Rat Race at Work

Need More Help with the Politics at Work?

100 Ways To Get On The Wrong Side Of Your Boss (And Strategies to Prevent You from Getting There!) was written for anyone who has ever been frustrated by his or her working relationship with the boss—and who hasn't ever felt this way! Bosses play a critically important role in your career success and getting on the wrong side of this important individual in your working life is not a good thing.

Each of these 100 Ways is designed to illustrate a particular problem that you may encounter when dealing with your boss and then an effective strategy to prevent this problem from reoccurring. You will learn how to deal more effectively with your boss in this fun and practical book filled with invaluable advice that can be utilized every day at work.

Written by Peter R. Garber, the author of *Winning the Rat Race at Work*, this book is a must read for anyone interested in getting ahead. You will want to keep a copy in your top desk drawer for ready reference whenever you find yourself in a challenging predicament at work.

ISBN: 1-895186-98-6   (paperback)
Also available in ebook formats. Order from your local bookseller, Amazon.com, or directly from the publisher at **http://www.InTroubleAtWork.com**

74 Tips for *Absolutely Great* **Teleconference Meetings**

Ida Shessel

Become a meeting superstar!

With the proliferation of teleconference meetings in today's distributed team environment, many organizations now conduct most of their meetings over the telephone. There are challenges associated with trying to ensure that these meetings are productive and successful.

74 Tips for Absolutely Great Teleconference Meetings contains tips for both the teleconference leader and the participant — tips on how to prepare for the teleconference, start the teleconference meeting and set the tone, lead the teleconference, keep participants away from their e-mail during the call, use voice and language effectively, and draw the teleconference to a close. The book also includes a helpful checklist you can use to assess what you need to do to make your teleconference meetings more effective.

Mastering the art of holding a good meeting is one sure-fire way to get recognized as a leader by your peers and your management. Being able to hold an *absolutely great* teleconference meeting positions you as a leader who can also leverage modern technologies to improve efficiency. Develop this career-building skill by ordering this book today!

Available in electronic formats from most ebook online retailers or directly from the publisher at **www.mmpubs.com**.

**77 Tips
for *Absolutely Great*
Meetings**

Ida Shessel

Make people *yearn* to attend your meetings!

Turn dull meetings into dynamic group experiences! Chances are that you spend a lot of time at meetings - some are focused and productive, while others are not. This ebook, written by a professional facilitator, contains 77 tips for both meeting leaders and participants. Implementing one or more of these tips can produce dramatic results at your meetings.

Learn how to strengthen your leadership abilities, plan effectively, use structure to get more from your meetings, manage group dynamics, empower yourself and others to become strong contributors to the meeting, and more. Inside this ebook there is even a helpful checklist that you can use to assess what you need to do to make your meetings more effective.

Our work life revolves around meetings - make yours the most effective they can be.

Available in electronic formats from most ebook online retailers or directly from the publisher at **http://www.mmpubs.com**.

273

Networking *for* Results

THE POWER *OF* PERSONAL CONTACT

In partnership with Michael J. Hughes, *The* Networking Guru, Multi-Media Publications Inc. has released a new series of books, ebooks, and audio books designed for business and sales professionals who want to get the most out of their networking events and help their career development.

Networking refers to the concept that each of us has a group or "network" of friends, associates and contacts as part of our on-going human activity that we can use to achieve certain objectives.

The *Networking for Results* series of products shows us how to think about networking strategically, and gives us step-by-step techniques for helping ourselves and those around us achieve our goals. By following these practices, we can greatly improve our personal networking effectiveness.

Visit **www.Networking-for-Results.com** for information on specific products in this series, to read free articles on networking skills, or to sign up for a free networking tips newsletter. Products are available from most book, ebook, and audiobook retailers, or directly from the publisher at **www.mmpubs.com.**

 **PM Audiobooks** The Project Management
Audio Library

In a recent CEO survey, the leaders of today's largest corporations identified project management as the top skillset for tomorrow's leaders. In fact, many organizations place their top performers in project management roles to groom them for senior management positions. Project managers represent some of the busiest people around. They are the ones responsible for planning, executing, and controlling most major new business activities.

Expanding upon the successful *Project Management Essentials Library* series of print and electronic books, Multi-Media Publications has launched a new imprint called the *Project Management Audio Library*. Under this new imprint, MMP is publishing audiobooks and recorded seminars focused on professionals who manage individual projects, portfolios of projects, and strategic programmes. The series covers topics including agile project management, risk management, project closeout, interpersonal skills, and other related project management knowledge areas.

This is not going to be just the "same old stuff" on the critical path method, earned value, and resource levelling; rather, the series will have the latest tips and techniques from those who are at the cutting edge of project management research and real-world application.

www.PM-Audiobooks.com